MINIMALISM FOR FAMILIES

Minimalist Living for Beginners via Frugal Living
and Simplify Your Life

(Simple Step by Step Guide on the Minimalist
Lifestyle)

D1808318

John Lorenz

Published by Tomas Edwards

© **John Lorenz**

All Rights Reserved

ISBN 978-1-989744-65-9

Legal & Disclaimer

The information contained in this book is not designed to replace or take the place of any form of medicine or professional medical advice. The information in this book has been provided for educational and entertainment purposes only.

The information contained in this book has been compiled from sources deemed reliable, and it is accurate to the best of the Author's knowledge; however, the Author cannot guarantee its accuracy and validity and cannot be held liable for any errors or omissions. Changes are periodically made to this book. You must consult your doctor or get professional medical advice before using any of the suggested remedies, techniques, or information in this book.

Table of Contents

Introduction

It has long been proven that any movement that is in trend causes many people to subconscious affection. For example, meditation, yoga or keto diet.

Minimalism entered the trend relatively recently. The word itself, like the concept as a whole, came from visual art. It originated in the US in the 60s. It has covered almost all branches of art, from fine and musical, and ending with an understanding of the architecture, design, and sense of space.

At some point of the end of the 20th century, as is often the case, the current began to go beyond the limits of art. Values of this kind began to penetrate ordinary life. Along with the rapid change of various subcultures that promote some particles of minimalism, the first evangelists of a simplified approach to life appeared.

Chapter 1: What Is Minimalism?

"It is the heart that makes a man rich. He is rich according to what he is, not according to what he was."

- Henry Ward Beecher

For me, minimalism is a way of living in which you only use and keep the items you need. This reduces stress and worry and helps you enjoy a better life. Nothing is worth losing your peace of mind and it is extremely relaxing not having to worry about your things all the time.

You also get to know yourself better as you can no longer have an identity based on your belongings and have more time with yourself. It forces you to focus on what really matters and not on distractions. It is a way of escaping the illusion that you have to buy things in order to be happy.

Going shopping or getting a new car might give you a momentary rush but it eventually fades away, leaving you in the position in which you were before buying it. If you were happy before purchasing such thing then you go back to that state but if you bought it thinking it was going to make you happy or solve your inner problems then you will find yourself with that void in your interior again, seeking to buy something else so it can fill it momentarily.

Living a minimalist life has a different meaning for different people. Minimalism begins in the mind, it is about owning only the items you need and love. It also goes past just items, it can expand to other areas of your life such as relationships, work and wealth. There is no definitive definition of minimalism since we all have different definitions and experiences with minimalism.

Here is one definition I really like by the minimalists (theminimalists.com/minimalism/) :

"Minimalism is a tool that can assist you in finding   freedom. Freedom from fear. Freedom from worry. Freedom   from   overwhelm. Freedom from guilt. Freedom from depression.   Freedom from the trappings of the consumer culture we've built our lives around.

That doesn't mean there's anything inherently wrong with owning material possessions. Today's problem seems to be the meaning we assign to our stuff: we tend to give too much meaning to our things,
often forsaking our health, our relationships, our passions, our personal growth, and our desire to contribute beyond ourselves."

The type of freedom that being a minimalist gives you is not easy to achieve by other means. The less stuff you own, the less things you have to worry about and take care of, the more time you have to yourself and your family and friends. The amount of things you need varies depending on who you are, this applies in different categories such as clothes, furniture, makeup and other material possessions. I have seen minimalists whose belongings fit in two luggages and still their makeup collection is 5 times the size of mine. Imagine that, everything she owns in this world fits in a carry on and a medium sized luggage and still her makeup items easily fill up half her carry on.

Let's use cars as example. A car is meant to carry people to different destinations, but having 5 cars in the parking lot does just the same thing, owning 5 cars won't get you to the destination faster but it will increase the amount of taxes and repairs you have to pay for. Whether the cars you have in your garage are Toyotas or Bugattis, you can't use more than one at the same time. Having one car may not only save fuel, but also provide an easy and quick decision the next day. Having 5 cars in your parking lot creates clutter in your mind. You can't instantly decide which car that you are going to use and you worry about maintaining all of them. Furthermore, the vehicles would still continue to depreciate as long as they continue to remain in the garage. I'm by no means hating on luxury or sports cars and if it makes you happy then you can go ahead and build your car collection but if this is not your situation, why don't you just buy and keep one car and save yourself from all these complications. Also, be careful when financing big purchases like this with credit. According to creditcards.com, 2 out of 3 Millennials doubt they'll ever be out of debt. This is a topic we will go back to in the finances chapter. Back to the cars, it's a different story when you live with someone else who needs a car on a daily basis because then you have your car and they have their own. One of the benefits of being a minimalist is to live stress free, so take a step forward to get rid of those things that are the source of your stress.

Many people strive towards being a minimalist, this makes sense as it has become a trend in the past few years. However, not many people have a clear concept of what being a minimalist means and that is partly because there is no clear definition. For some people it means living in a desolate area or in their van with limited belongings while for others it means living in their own house with minimal decoration and items. While it would be fun to live in a van and travel everywhere, I'm more of a house type of minimalist. Which one would do you consider yourself as? Being a minimalist doesn't require that you only own 20 items total, you can have as many items as you want as long as they make you happy and that you actually appreciate and use each one of them. The amount of things that every person chooses to own depends entirely on that person and his or her self knowledge and can vary as that person goes through different stages in their life.

Chapter 2: Benefits Of Minimalism

Becoming a minimalist provides opportunities that you have been missing before. Each benefit ties into each other, so it is not that you work toward one, but rather that you gain them all as you declutter. Some benefits may come more easily to you depending on how ready you are to accept the minimalist mindset. Other benefits may not be as essential to your life as certain gains listed. Think through the mindset and the benefits to decide your starting point and your goal.

Freedom

Freedom can be described regarding financial and personal peace. It also relates to being freer to do the things you love.

Being materialistic can hamper you. You tend to buy things, even if there is no clear reason. You might think, "Perhaps that will go well on the mantle" or "I have space for a new picture on the wall." These tendencies prevent us from being free to enjoy the things we love.

From a financial perspective, hobbies and travel are expensive. If you spend $3, $6, or $10 here and there or every day, you compromise affording hobbies and travel. Consider the coffee dilemma. Let's say you work near a place that offers you $3 drinks, whether it is a coffee, latte, chai latte or tea. You work four days a week. Each day you work, you buy a $3 chai latte, which means you spend $12 per week. You spend $48 per month. At the end of the year, you have spent $576 on chai lattes.

Now consider a warehouse store. At one store you can spend $7.98 for ninety-six fluid ounces of chai. A twenty-ounce chai latte is ten ounces of chai and ten ounces of milk. You will get about ten days of chai lattes from a purchase at a warehouse store. You could even decide to go with five ounces of chai per drink versus ten to get twenty days of chai . If you only drink it four times a week, then you have five weeks' worth of chai lattes. What could you do with the savings? You could fly to a new destination. You could spend that money on your hobby. You could pay off a debt that is worrisome. Above all, you could gain financial freedom to do more of the things you love.

Time is another factor of freedom. What if you need to keep working to afford the credit card payments? Some jobs offer paid time off for vacations, but if you keep spending money can you afford to go? You may figure out that you need a second source of income versus a holiday to pay off your debts.

Your time may also be filled with shopping and other time-consuming tasks preventing you from feeling free. Minimalism is not just about materialistic items but also about how much of your time is filled with useless or unnecessary tasks.

Keep freedom and time in mind as you read about other benefits.

Worry-Free Living

Spending money causes stress. Agonizing over the things you cannot afford to do or do not have time for can eat away at you. Minimalizing your life gives you the opportunity to have peace of mind. You will become less stressed and worried because you are decluttering your life of the trappings that make you fearful.

What is causing you to worry now? Are you wondering where you will come up with the next mortgage payment? Is your credit card debt over $10,000, maybe closer to $30,000? Do you wonder how you will get one child to their extra-curricular activity without making your other child late?

Maybe you look around your home and think, "When will I have the time to organize and clean?" You might look at a book you want to read and have no idea when you can do something for yourself like read that book.

Stress is something we create for ourselves, so if we adopt a minimalist lifestyle, we can let go of the worry and stress. We can make peace with the things we cannot do as a way to enjoy the things that are possible.

You cannot buy peace of mind, but you can attain it through minimalism and live a happier life.

Health

When you are stress-free and you gain time for yourself, your health improves. Health is a mental and physical concept. Physically, your health gets better when you put more focus into exercising, eating correctly, and getting rid of debilitating habits. Mentally, you gain health because you are worry free. Your fear and stress dissipate.

What would you do if you had an hour to yourself? If you didn't worry about cleaning, where the kids need to go next, or how to pay a bill? How free would you feel? Studies show the minimalist lifestyle improves health because you can relax, unwind, and focus on what is most essential—your health.

Focus

How well are you focusing when you have a million tasks? We like to think we can multi-task, but what we do is switch-task, not always finishing something before moving on. Can you type on a computer and talk at the same time? Try it. Did you just type something you said versus the thought you meant to type? Of course, because you are trying to split your focus. When you have less to think about, you have more focus on the tasks at hand.

Our brains can compartmentalize to sharpen our focus. When you are at work—doing your best—do you bring your personal life with you? No, you cannot for fear of losing your job. You have to leave your worries behind and get the work accomplished. Decluttering your life allows you to do this. You have fewer worries, you find more time, and your health is better; therefore, you can focus more on what matters most to you and the tasks you need to complete.

Less Fear of Failure

Fear of failure comes from having too much to do and no time or focus to make it happen. You see how each of these benefits ties into one another? They do not tie in a linear way, but in multiple pathways. By restructuring your life, you not only gain freedom, a less stressful experience, and more focus, but you also do not have to fear the consequences.

What if you:

● Put your entire monthly income toward your debts, groceries, mortgage, and utilities;

● Have no money left for fun;

● Are left with debts that are more than you can pay each month;

● End up in foreclosure and bankruptcy.

This what-if statement is just an example of what you might consider a lifetime failure. Other fears can include failing your children or your spouse, or to obtain the goals you have. When your mind is full of worry, you lack proper health, and you have no time for yourself or others, you feel like a failure. But, you do not have to feel this way. Leave all of these thoughts behind by minimizing the things in life you don't need and go after what is essential.

Decluttering

A step toward minimalism is decluttering. You streamline your life to fit your goals. You get rid of things that you have not used in the last six months. You buy only what is necessary. In your home you can gain more room, or you can downsize to a smaller, less worrisome home. In this way, you lower your carbon footprint in the world.

Regaining Values

The last benefit to discuss deals directly with the larger world problems. There is a general shift in thought with people thinking they are entitled from the moment they are born. They are entitled to own huge properties, earn $100,000 a year, and have vacations. But, are you?

Let's consider values throughout history. Yes, some individuals took property and goods through legal means, such as fighting to overtake someone else's property. Some religious people stole money in the name of their religion and used that money for their gain and not to help others. But, despite the bad deeds of some people, the majority of people understood that to have anything you must work for it.

This is still true today. It might take twenty years to earn vacation for someone. For another person, they may live paycheck to paycheck but are happier than the person who consistently makes more but never has anything to show for it besides material items.

By regaining values and realizing that if you work hard, you will be happy and gain what is essential to you, your life will improve. The minimalist mindset teaches us to discover our values.

Chapter 3: Minimalism Meets Decluttering

Decluttering, Decoded

Decluttering is the resulting action you take for wanting to clear out your bedroom drawers, your entire home, your work schedule, your mental space, or all aspects of your life. You may need to relocate to another city, wish to consolidate your possessions after getting married, or simply let go of belongings that you no longer find useful.

Decluttering can also arise from a shift in your perspective in life – a loved one may have recently passed and you realize that the things he or she had left behind are not necessarily the things you would want to keep for yourself or even pass on to your kids. It can even be the result of your being overwhelmed by the large number of belongings that are holding you back from living your life to the fullest.

You might think decluttering is something you perform as a one-time, big-time activity that simply involves getting rid of barely worn clothes and other dispensable stuff. But the truth is that you do a one-big-purge only if you make sure to maintain decluttering in your life.

Road to Minimalism

The good news is that the act of constantly decluttering will help steer you toward learning about and practicing minimalism. You will observe within yourself a significant shift in how you perceive each aspect of your life. You start noticing how more at peace you feel at home since you deliberately kept clutter from creeping onto surfaces and into corners. You learn to appreciate how effortless it is for you to throw on an outfit every single morning and know that you look great in it.

Decluttering makes you feel like breathing much easier, knowing that your list of activities for the day consists only of essential tasks. It helps you figure out that you only need simple things to feed your body so that you look and feel confident in your own skin. Decluttering also allows you to let go of unnecessary things that clutter your mind and fill it instead with clarity. Ultimately, you discover the beauty in having less in order to live more. You start seeing the joy in not having to fill your home with all kinds of trinkets, your time with uncalled-for commitments, and your mind with pointless thoughts.

In the end, decluttering leads you to practicing minimalism in your life.

You are living in a world that is constantly enticing you to want to have more, which eggs you on to buy more. Advertisements come at you and make you believe you will only feel satisfied with yourself if you keep getting more stuff. But every purchase actually makes you feel more mentally and emotionally loaded, eventually causing you to lose the freedom to spend time on the things that actually matter to you and that bring value and fulfillment to your life.

Slave No More

Minimalism enables you to get rid of the things you do not need in your life. It helps you see the sensibility in giving up those worthless knickknacks you have been storing in your treasure chest all these years. It allows you to reclaim valuable spaces that you can fill with stuff that you truly need to live your life to the fullest.

Practicing the minimalist lifestyle helps you remember that you become a slave to the material things that you get attached to. You end up wasting precious time cleaning and organizing all the things you have accumulated, time that you could have used in pursuing our passions and realizing your goals. This is the reason a minimalist feels happy when he sees his cabinets and drawers are empty – it means he has eliminated the stuff that do not help him achieve his dreams.

No Strings Attached

Minimalism helps you let go of being attached to your possessions, which is a big reason you find it difficult to throw away stuff. This is especially true for things that make you remember particular times or experiences in your life. But living the minimalist way reminds you of the fact that your mind holds the memories that you share with family and friends, not your belongings. Minimalism helps you realize that, instead of dwelling in the past, you are better off looking forward to what the future holds for you. Rather than forming an attachment to your treasures and trinkets, you should be forming bonds with people.

Order In the Court

Being a minimalist drives home why it makes sense to keep your home decluttered and organized. It helps you see the importance of making sure each item you own has a specific use as well as a particular space to store it. Everything becomes easier when you know where something is every single time because you keep it one place only.

Sitting Un-Pretty No More

Minimally is extremely helpful when it comes to curbing your spending. It teaches you to always purchase things with care to avoid buying anything that do not serve a purpose or add value to your life. Minimalism also something has to go each time you buy new stuff and bring it into your home. Things you will have to let go, either by donating or selling, includes those that simply sit and gather dust.

Life, Simplified

Because minimalism promotes getting rid of material things that are not necessary in your life, it encourages you to also:

•Lean towards digitization: Enjoy the convenience of scanning photos into a memory drive or a computer, then throwing away the photos themselves. You can also make use of technology in creating photo albums, letters, tickets, and invoices.

•Multitask with technology: You can still accomplish all the things you need to do without having to use a desktop computer, a laptop, a tablet, a cellphone, and a music player. You can definitely make do with just one or two devices.

•Limit information consumption: With you getting exposed to floods of stimulation all through your day, it is no wonder why you end up losing focus on the information you should truly care about. Minimalism helps you avoid becoming lost in the world of consumerism and being updated on the important stuff going on across the globe instead.

•Prioritize your commitments: Adopting the minimalist lifestyle steers you towards accomplishing more things by using your time wisely, rather than wasting it unproductive meetings or dates. It helps you learn simply refuse to do or participate in something if you know it would not be of value to you.

•Place emphasis on experiences: Minimalism helps you see the joy in having more experiences instead of material possessions.

•Take charge of your thoughts: Living the minimalist way makes you see the significance of controlling your mind and concentrating on the things that truly matter to you as you strive for emotional balance as well.

Chapter 4: The Efficacy Of Minimalism

Minimalism is, in essence, paying more attention to those things that are the most essential to us and doing away with pointless distractions. The notion has immense worth simply because there are a number of things that sidetrack us, taking our eyes off what we want. The minimalist dogma balances that of effective altruism, even though altruistic intents nurtured by many don't see any fruition due to limitations in finance and maybe time. In this chapter, we will point out minimalistic ways to liberate time and money, and at the same time, improve one's quality of life.

Minimalism vs. Consumerism

Minimalism is a clear pointer of the things that are essential and valuable. Having possession of less quantifiable things, however, does not necessarily make a comfortable definition for being a minimalist.

The central theme lies in how one holds dear what is termed essential to life, letting go of only having things for the sake of owning them and effectively modifying the connotations one bestows to quantifiable properties.

A minimalist effectively discards the mistaken idea that true happiness is attained by giving attention to quantifiable properties, as against focusing one's energies on the rewards of knowledge and experience.

Such accountable and supportable consumption allows one to save more on valuable resources- energy, money, time, etc. and by so doing, enjoy some of the best things in life.

In being discerning about what quantifiable properties one owns, a person can well ensure that he/she has a practical workspace which, in turn, implies that there would be more motivation during working hours.

Answer the following questions as honestly as you can

What connotations do you attach to quantifiable properties?

What value do you place on quantifiable properties when it comes to the pursuit of happiness?

How can having less stuff, yet having more time, money and energy on your hands translate to a happier life?

Minimalism vs. Monies

Minimalism does not in any way imply being in a state of poverty, going hungry, continually living with scarcity, or being miserly. It means recognizing what it is that one needs and continuing well within one's means, often managing resources more deliberately in the process.

A minimalist, however, doesn't automatically expend less than other people. Instead, tremendous effort is put into jettisoning consumerist cravings, and this is done without relinquishing one's overall urges, choosing instead to expend cash on the possessions that really add value to their life.

For instance, one could love traveling as a way of discovering nature and unwinding. So, his/her spending could be rightly guided so that scarce resources get to be channeled on elevating experiences that will be long-lasting.

Minimalism is often about growing a particular focus on being affluent in experience rather than in material goods.

Answer the following questions as honestly as you can

What do you feel is the relationship between minimalism and money?

What value do you place on experience?

How has your experiences sharpened your outlook to life as against simply owning things?

Minimalism vs. Order

A well put together life implies a well put together mind. Order remains a vital tool in our lives, but not many people realize this until its benefit finally accompanies each experience in their lives.

With minimalism, one gets to embrace order in everyday living. That is, in a bodily sense, as it implies that one would have to cut down on the imaginative fumes that would stand to prevent the creation of a space that evenly reflects one's individuality, without compromising passions or aesthetic preferences.

It is essential to be surrounded by things that genuinely communicate with one's individuality, which serves purpose; this is an excellent way to center oneself. Crafting effective collaboration between the individual and professional spaces can go a long way in helping to ease apprehensions and help promote comfort.

Putting order in place enables more organization in our workspaces, making sure that we can meet every deadline more efficiently, creating timetables that work.

Answer the following questions as honestly as you can

What do you feel is the role of order when it comes to being effective?

What has order done to your overall efficiency as a person?

How can order and minimalism be tools in achieving a happier life?

Minimalism vs. Vocation

Minimalism supports the philosophy of mindfulness; a minimalist will often find it convenient to flexibly expand on his mental space. This action enhances the overall clarity of mind, which plays a useful role in decision making.

Applying minimalism as a lifestyle choice can immensely impact on vocation-related decisions — this includes options of whether or not to go for specific job offers in which you find more fulfillment or merely seeing in your mind's eye what innovations you'd like to make in your field of choice.

In coming to terms with what one can refer to as the most central in life, one can unmistakably weigh what it is that will test one's abilities, or what situations will be most suitable for efficiency; this would in turn aid reaffirmation of one's actual values.

Exercise

Answer the following questions as honestly as you can

What do you make of making career choices based on the principles of minimalism?

How does one maintain efficiency if he/she chooses a career path based on minimalism?

How effective is minimalism in the general productivity of individuals who practice it?

Minimalism vs. Output

The basic concept of minimalism is bound to breed productivity as it adequately does away with distractions, wasteful disbursement of energies that could be otherwise channeled, cloning more efficiency on a day-to-day basis.

With this lifestyle choice, one focuses all of his/her energy on carefully selected tasks, giving the needed attention to the most serious issues and responding adequately to emerging responsibilities. This act helps to promote professionalism while catering to one's happiness at the same time. It also helps in forgoing the urge to overwhelm one's schedule with errands that may not have any real influence on constructive outcomes; also inspiring one to wisely channel his/her time.

The rationalization of one's methodology has proven to aid communication more successfully between both facets of life-that is the professional and private facets.

Answer the following questions as honestly as you can

Do you think minimalism can effectively boost your productivity? How so?

Point out how effective output in professionalism can be credited to being a minimalist

Can you elaborate on how distractions and excessive wastage can be managed in your work place?

Minimalism vs. Existentialism

It is important to groom healthy relationships and establish newer connections; this, for most people, is fundamental to life.

Healthy relationships strengthen us, bringing happiness into our lives and aiding us to develop as individuals. By engaging ourselves with people of high positivity, who respect or maybe even share our values, we are able to steady our thoughts and minds, getting the best out of every link we make.

It is not too hard to get a 'no' from a minimalist, once he/she perceives toxicity in any connection or link. This also implies that he/she would always find the strength to break off ties with anybody that seems to be absorbing precious energy. The reason for such drastic actions is because a true minimalist realizes how vital it is to preserve strength for other meaningful relationships that would invariably sustain and develop them.

This disposition can also benefit our relationships at work too, as it implies that we get to dedicate more time to the discussions that hold meaning and pass a lesser amount of time feeling insecure of where it is we stand.

Answer the following questions as honestly as you can

Do you think it is important to constantly nurture newer relationships? Why?

How has cutting off ties with toxic relationships helped your overall productivity?

It is important to note here that the key is not to cut off as many relationships as possible but to rather embrace those that provide value (Love, happiness, entertainment and growth etc.) without toxicity.

Minimalism vs. well-being

Minimalists, as they prioritize positivity, never lose sight of living happily and freely. They endeavor to keep an active link between body and mind.

The more streamlined and joyful a life we nurture, the more liberty we will experience to make choices based entirely on what it is that we need. This conceptual liberty makes a more peaceful mind space where the best considerations are made for our next phases.

This peaceful mind space, in both profession and personal living, is birthed by the outputs of the minimalist lifestyle. For example, a minimalist mindset inspires people to embrace the moment — recouping time and energy for our exclusive benefit. This liberty further pursues the promotion of ingenuity over ingestion, appetite over assets, which in the long run provides positive effects on our general well-being- that is, physical and mental. In purging our minds, while also consolidating our physical wellbeing, we are able to merge both our personal and professional sphere of influence — giving us ample time and space to mature as individuals unrestricted by the demands of society.

Answer the following questions as honestly as you can

Please elaborate on the idea of minimalism contributing significantly to one's well-being

Is the mental space prone to more efficiency if one cuts down on excesses? How so?

What limitations does a person have to deal with if the body and the mind aren't properly merged in terms of professional and personal spheres?

Chapter 5: De-Cluttering

One of the biggest reasons why people are drawn to minimalism is because of the idea of living a lifestyle free of clutter. Modern society has us believing that we are only as good as what we own, so we tend to acquire a lot of new belongings so that we can stay relevant. Often, we fail to get rid of old belongings because they are usually not even that old. As well, they tend to serve as symbols of our time, since they were acquired with money and money requires us to invest time into earning it. In many instances the time we invested in earning the money was not enjoyed, therefore it can end up being viewed negatively.

Learning to effectively de-clutter your life is important. It allows you to break emotional attachments to material belongings you already own, which can also make it easier to prevent you from generating emotional attachments to any newer objects. You will begin to view objects as mere objects which can make it easier to keep yourself from acquiring anything else unnecessary in the future.

This chapter is going to walk you through the process of de-cluttering your life in effective and simple manners. Each tip will teach you how you can de-clutter without ever leading yourself into a position of lack or need. Remember, minimalism is not about living with virtually nothing, it is about living without the belongings that we do not need to lead a happy and fulfilling lifestyle. You might be shocked to realize how little you actually need to thrive in a happy lifestyle, but once you find out you will likely never look back.

Tip #6: Reducing Instead of Eliminating

For some things, you might look at them and go "I can't get rid of that!" and this is completely natural. Clothes, dishes, utensils, and other such things you won't want to get rid of because they are important parts of your life. However, it is a good idea to take a look at them and see how much you actually need.

Often, we hoard a vast number of things we don't need. We keep clothes we will only wear one season out of the year, or that we may only wear once in a while. We keep several dishes, despite not all of them being used on a regular basis. We keep tons of toiletries, but only use a few. You get the idea. When you can't completely eliminate something from your life, try reducing the amount that you own. Find ways that you can eliminate the excess, and keep what you absolutely need.

Remember, minimalism isn't all about getting rid of everything and living with a lack. It is about getting rid of the excess and living with only what you need. There is no point in earning money and spending time on belongings you will never need in the long run, or that you will never use. Instead, sell, or donate them and open up the space in your life.

Tip #7: Your Wardrobe

Our wardrobes tend to become massive, featuring a large number of excess items we don't ever use. They say that there are 52 seasons in fashion, and many people can attest to this by looking in their wardrobe. The number of items we keep in our wardrobes can be stressful. We have to store them, organize them, maintain them, and often we find ourselves adding more without even thinking about it. The amount of time we invest in maintaining our wardrobe is enormous. Never mind how much time we later spend trying decide on what we want to wear and what to accessorize it with. It can become overwhelming and can lead to a great amount of stress and wasted time.

Cleaning your wardrobe should be one of the first things you tackle. It might be difficult to whittle it down to a manageable size, but you will find it is one of the most cathartic activities you might ever do along your minimalist journey. Releasing our wardrobe of the excess and narrowing it down to what we actually like and wear gives us the opportunity to save time and get focused. You no longer have to spend as much time maintaining your wardrobe or deciding what you would like to wear each day. Instead, you can pay attention to what you have and put it together effortlessly. Once you know your wardrobe well, you will find it extremely easy to wear anything you want.

Something many minimalists try to do is the 33 item challenge. This means that you eliminate everything except for 33 items. These items include jewelry, shoes, socks, underwear, pants, shirts, sweaters, and jackets. Narrowing it down this small can be hard, but it can also be satisfying. It means that you have less to maintain and worry about. Also, you'll be surprised how many outfits you can create out of 33 items.

Tip #8: Charity Box

Throughout your minimalist journey you are going to want to have a charity box handy. This is where you are going to throw everything that you no longer want to keep. You can use it for your wardrobe, for your pantry, your kitchen items, toiletries, and more. Always make sure that you aren't throwing crappy junk away into this box, as no one likes having to sort through a charity box that has been filled with trash. However, add as much as you would like so that you can give most of your things away. This makes it easy for you to eliminate things from your life without hassle.

Once you have eliminated virtually everything from your home, you should continue to keep a small charity box handy. This will give you the opportunity to eliminate things as they are needing to be eliminated, instead of holding onto it because it is too difficult for you to go about donating it. Once your box is filled, go ahead and donate it and start a new one.

Tip #9: 6-Month Box Challenge

This challenge is an excellent way to discover whether you actually want to keep something or not. First, you want to put everything that you are questioning into a box. A dress you may not fit anymore, a camera you were going to learn to use, and anything else that you have been putting off but keeping "just in case". Put all of these items that you struggle to let go of into a box. Date the box, seal it, and put it away in your closet. Six months from the date that you seal the box, if you have not felt the need to use anything, go ahead and get rid of it all!

You can do this as many times as you want or need to, though you will likely find that over time it is no longer needed as you become more disciplined in not bringing home things you do not need anymore. It is an excellent way to discover whether you actually want to keep something or if you are just keeping it for unnecessary attachments that you have yet to break.

Tip #10: "Just in Case"

We all have a tendency to keep items "just in case" we need them. We keep medicine "just in case" we get a headache, we keep several sets of guest towels "just in case" we have company over, we keep several pairs of sheets "just in case" we need them, several extra dishes "just in case" we choose to entertain, and so on and so forth. The amount of excess we keep "just in case" is really quite impressive, but that doesn't mean that we should keep holding onto it.

Look, you may or may not find that you need to use something once every six months. And sure, having it available to you is great, but having to store it in between is not always so wonderful. Imagine all of the things that you are holding onto for "just in case" times. If you were to eliminate them, you would have so much more free space! These items should be eliminated. Let go of them! If you are really struggling, try the six-month box challenge with them. Otherwise, just let them go. If you find that you need an item every now and again, find someone you can borrow it off of. Or, if it's something that can be bought as a multi-tool so that you can get rid of several individual pieces, learn to condense your items. This makes it significantly easier for you to store things.

Tip #11: Sentimental Items

Sentimental items can be the hardest of all when it comes to eliminating belongings for your minimalist journey. You might think "not that! So and so gave it to me, and I could never let it go!" and fair enough, many items have a very strong meaning to us. If it's something that genuinely brings you joy or that you get use from on a regular basis, then of course there is no need to let it go. However, many times we hold onto sentimental belongings in the back of our closet because we're too guilty to let them go, given their history. We think, "oh no, so and so gave me that. I never use it, but I can't get rid of it either."

If you dig a little deeper, you likely have no valid reason as to why you can't get rid of it, either. You might feel guilty about the idea of getting rid of something that meant a lot to someone else you care about, or because someone gave it to you with great intentions and that is something you want to hold onto. But, if you think about it logically, items do not carry memories or emotions, people do. You can easily remember any memory you want to, whether or not you have a physical attachment to the item. If you really don't want to forget it, try taking a photograph of it and saving it on a digital cloud somewhere, then eliminating the item itself. This can help keep the memory of it alive while eliminating the belonging from your home.

Tip #12: Your Car

When you are minimizing your belongings, you need to think about your car. Our cars become mobile waste bins for everything. We leave garbage, bottles, bags, clothes, shoes, and more in our cars because it's easier. Then, we forget they are in there and they don't get used or cleaned up for what seems like forever. It's important that you stay on top of your car and keep it clean and clear of chaos.

The first step is to completely eliminate everything from your car and give it a good vacuum. You want to clean it thoroughly from the inside out and make sure that nothing is left behind. Get underneath your seats, in the trunk, and even underneath your mats. Clean your entire car up so that it is completely empty, and then go ahead and put it back together.

Two things you might consider carrying in your car are: a trash bag or basket, and a catch-all basket. A catch-all basket allows you to throw items like bottles, clothes, shoes, and other odds and ends into the basket. Then, you can simply bring the basket inside and sort it into where it needs to go. This will keep you organized and keep your car clean, making it easier for you to stay focused and mindful over your car space.

Tip #13: Digitizing Belongings

There are many belongings we have that can be digitized, and it is highly recommended. Digitizing your belongings means that they will take up significantly less space, as they are all put into a cloud-storage instead of physical storage. There are many things that you can digitize to make it easier for you to manage.

Photographs, music, movies, books, notebooks, recipes, shopping lists, phone numbers and addresses, scrapbooks, and more can all be turned into digital copies. By doing so, you eliminate the number of belongings you have to store physically, and make it easier for you to bring everything around with you. You should always back up your digital files to prevent yourself from losing anything. Cloud storage is often the most reliable form, but you should also consider an external storage device such as a USB stick or an external hard drive for extra security.

Tip #14: Borrow

There are many things we purchase that could instead be borrowed. Instead of spending your money on buying something and finding a space to store it, consider borrowing. You can borrow books, tools, ingredients, and often even larger things such as vehicles when you are in need. There is no need to purchase something that you are not going to use on a regular basis.

With minimalism becoming much more popular, you can often find sites online where people have items you can borrow from them. These sites allow you to type in what you are looking for and where you are looking and will pull up results so that you can borrow from others instead of purchasing the items yourself. This saves money, time, and space.

Tip #15: Minimize Electronics

So many people own several electronics these days. Cell phones, music devices, computers, television sets, cable boxes, video game devices, and more are all purchased and then stored around the house. Even kitchen electronics such as blenders, crockpots, microwaves, toaster ovens and other smaller devices are hoarded. These items can take up a lot of space, and they are costly. In many cases, items like cell phones, televisions, video game systems and computers are taking up money without even being in use. We have them hooked up to monthly subscription services that enable us to have massive amounts of data, access to games, television and music, and more. If we take an honest look at our electronics, we likely only have a couple of favorites and the rest sit around collecting dust and wasting money.

If you want to make the most of your money, time, and space, you should minimize your electronics. Keep items that can do everything, and get rid of the rest.

There is no need to own a tablet, computer, music device, and cell phone. Instead, keep your cell phone and computer and leave the rest. In most cases, we own way too many electronic devices simply because they look cool and they may have one or two extra features that we feel would be valuable for us. In reality, we do not actually need them and they simply take up space and cost us money.

Tip #16: One Size Fits All

Condensing items into "one size fits all" or "multi-use" items is an extremely beneficial way to reduce the number of items you own and still keep all of the value that you had gained from your items. Consider something as simple as a multi-tool hammer. In many hardware stores you can find a hammer that doubles as a screw driver and even pliers as well. This means that you can eliminate several of your tools and tool bits and simply keep the one item. With that item, you can accomplish anything you desire and it is extremely easy to store it. There is no need to have a massive tool box, you simply need one single tool.

There are many items in your house that can be condensed to serve a single purpose. You can find kitchen items, bathroom items, storage units, and other devices that are multi-use and allow you to eliminate several individual items while replacing them with just one. For a minimalist, this type of item is like a dream come true.

Tip #17: Buy Experiences

Instead of investing in items that are going to bring about a few moments of joy, invest in experiences that are going to bring about years of joy. This is one of the greatest secrets, and joys, of being a minimalist.

Most people invest in items and they feel a short amount of joy. They purchase the item and feel joy as they are purchasing it, and then they feel joy the first few times they use it, if they use it. You have likely heard the phrase "the novelty wore off" when people are talking about their new belongings. This phrase, and action, is extremely common. In fact, the more people consume, the shorter the "novelty" period lasts and the less joy they gain from the items they buy. They may even reach a point where they feel instant regret because they invested money into something they knew they didn't really need or want overall.

Investing in experiences is almost always a sure-fire way to gain the greatest joy out of the money you are spending. You gain so many things when you invest in an experience, aside from just the experience itself. You also gain memories, knowledge, joy, and more. These results are something that you simply cannot purchase over the counter at any store.

Tip #18: One in, One Out

A great rule that many minimalists live by is called "one in, one out". This means that any time you purchase something and bring it home, you must get rid of something else. This keeps you from bringing home several things without being mindful of it. You become more aware of the space you have and where you want to store things, and you learn that in many cases, what you wanted to bring in was not actually that important. It helps encourage you to become more mindful over your shopping, and your cluttering habits.

You should use the one in, one out rule with anything you are bringing into your house. This allows you to keep your space organized, and prevents you from piling things up. Often we clutter our houses without realizing we are doing so because we aren't thinking about the space we have, but rather we are thinking about the instantaneous joy we could have from bringing a new item home. As a result, we end up drowning in clutter. The one in, one out rule helps you eliminate this habit.

De-cluttering is one of the biggest reasons why people are drawn to minimalism. They see an opportunity to live a lifestyle that is free of excess and junk, and they are excited to jump on board. This is a major part of minimalism, and de-cluttering your house and your life is a great way to get started. Remember, minimalism is much more than this. However, having a good, clutter-free foundation is the best way to keep yourself from becoming overwhelmed with too much stuff and to help you along your way as a minimalist.

Chapter 6: You Do Not Need To Be Bogged Down With "Stuff."

So just what is a minimalistic way of life? Why is this a lot more than a technique to décor? What does it truly suggest?

" Get all you desire, by finding you currently have it ...".

Basically, a minimalist way of life merely suggests minimizing the clutter, downsizing your belongings, and intending to do more with less. It implies valuing a couple of things rather than having a big quantity of clutter that you do not truly require or desire.

We frequently see minimalism as an approach to UI design for devices from firms like Apple and on an increasing variety of sites. Here, the necessary maxim to follow is 'communicate, do not decorate.' That indicates that unless something is serving a real function, it does not belong in the design.

A site does not require a patterned background, it does not require unneeded menus, and it does not thrive by filling every bit of white area. Every component ought to serve a function, whether that is to direct the viewers' eyes in a specific direction, to communicate some essential information, or to help with a crucial interaction. If a button does not do anything, it does not have to be there!

Bringing Minimal Design Into Your Home

This identical attitude can then be applied to décor. Naturally, you do not have to convey anything as such when it pertains to your home's design, however, you can achieve something comparable when taking a look at items of furnishings, and so on.

Minimalist items of furnishings are products that are practical as they do not have lines or decor that does not have to be there. That suggests that they are going to be comprised of straight lines, and they will not have things like swirly handles, or needlessly fancy feet. It all serves a function.

With that working as the basis for your design, you can then continue with that standard idea by including simply a couple of items that you require while keeping away from the temptation to include additional decor that is going to serve no genuine purpose (naturally we'll be going over how to do all this in following chapters).

In UI and design, this minimalist idea has actually come forward due to the fact that it enables much better interactions. By having less disruptive components, this method has the ability to better direct users to the ideal points on the screen and motivate the appropriate interactions. It additionally permits a site design to better scale to various screen sizes when users use different devices, and it creates more room that makes the experience more relaxing and pleasurable.

However, while your home is not a UI, all these identical principles apply just the same. When you begin getting rid of unneeded decors and clutter, you begin to make engaging with your home much easier. When there are less things on your desk, you'll discover that you can locate what you desire that much more promptly and quickly.

Also, when there is less clutter in your interior decoration, you'll have less clutter in your visual field. This is going to make your area that much more soothing and peaceful and additionally make it a lot easier to keep it orderly.

And that, in turn, implies you're now investing less time cleaning and less time digging around for things. Your house is going to be clean and appealing more frequently, and you'll have more energy and time to do the important things that you take pleasure in doing!

Much like a UI, your home serves a purpose. That purpose is to support the way of life that you wish to live. So, if a thing in your house is not serving that function, then the answer is to remove it! And after that, you can breathe more easily.

Minimalism as a Response to Materialism

A growing number of individuals are beginning to understand the advantages of, in fact, having less clutter and less things and this is leading to a circumstance where they are better off with only a couple of gorgeous items instead of feeling the requirement to head out and purchase all they see promoted on TV.

And what does that cause as a result? Greater fulfillment and joy with less things! This makes a huge distinction since it implies that you're now going to be more pleased and invest less time considering the things that you do not have.

And you'll have more cash to invest in those select couple of products and on the important things that actually make you pleased.

This is the best remedy to our contemporary, materialistic culture, and it is additionally the very same approach that has actually been preached by various philosophies and spiritual practices for centuries. Joy does not originate from what you own. It originates from what you do with what you own.

You could be the wealthiest individual on the planet, yet be extremely stressed out and dissatisfied. Why? Due to the fact that you have actually developed a way of life that still presses the limits of your budget plan. You have actually been accustomed to a particular lifestyle that costs a great deal of cash and includes a great deal of hard work.

Keeping this way of life takes a great deal of effort, and yet you are still constantly considering the things that you do not have and the things you desire. You do not stop to take a minute to take pleasure in the important things you have, and things of unbelievable worth that are already there wind up being lost in all the noise and losing their worth to you.

Minimalism has to do with getting the most out of what you have, and this applies to your private life. Taking an appreciation mindset implies getting up and feeling so fortunate that you're with your partner. It suggests being thrilled with your kids and with your health and with your flexibility. It implies not looking next door and wanting that you had the next-door neighbor's widescreen TV. It suggests not squandering cash on scrap, and it indicates being present.

And naturally, minimalism suggests that your joy isn't bound in physical belongings. It indicates that you can get pleasure out your own mind and your own body, instead of letting that little scratch on your vehicle destroy your day.

Life is there to be indulged in, and there is a lot out there to be savored today. If all you can think about is just how much you desire the most recent toy or gizmo though, then you're not going to have time to stop and take pleasure in those things. You need to work harder, remain in the workplace later, and get loans.

However, what you do not understand is that you currently have all you require. It's time to unwind and enjoy it!

Lots of philosophers concur that this is the secret to joy. To be able to really value things and let go off unneeded tension, sidetracking desires, and that gnawing sense of discontentment.

Obviously, in a capitalist world, where every business under the sun is continuously flaunting its products, this could be extremely tough. Luckily, you have this book to hand, which is going to assist you in getting all you desire by finding that you currently have it.

Chapter 7: Introduction To Minimalism

This first chapter is going to give you the basic principles and ideas of what minimalism is and where it came from. When you have the basic information, you can start your journey on the best possible footing.

Many people confuse the term 'minimalism' with interior decoration or something similar but it's more than just deciding not to have a lot of furniture in your living room! Minimalism in so many ways is about an intention. You are telling yourself that you are going to live your best life with only the things that you really need. You're not going to clutter your life or space with the things that aren't necessary for your health or wellbeing, and instead, you're going to concentrate on necessities.

Let's break it down a little further.

What is Minimalism?

Minimalism is an intention and a promise to yourself, but it comes from within and has nothing to do with outside influences. By choosing a minimalistic lifestyle, you are opting to only own or have the things which you need in your life, which bring you value, and to throw out or cast away anything which causes a distraction. It is a way of thinking and a core value which brings improvements to your entire life.

For instance, minimalism helps you see the world differently, and it helps you to value things so much more as a result.

This isn't to say that you can't own nice things, of course, you can, but you would question whether or not you really need them, before deciding to make that purchase. This also comes down to the relationships in your life. You would not clutter your life with friendships that aren't necessary, and instead, you would stick to nurturing connections which bring something useful and meaningful.

By clearing out your life in this way, both physically and mentally, you are freeing up space in your brain for value and meaning. It isn't about needing to own the latest gadget or the most up to date label of jeans, it's about knowing that what you have is what you need without having to copy or duplicate someone else.

The most important thing to realise about minimalism is that it comes from within and it is not something which can be chosen without intention. A person who begins to live a minimalistic lifestyle needs to make the choice with intention, and they need to know why they're doing it. It's so easy to be seduced by what we think we need, or by a desire to live up to standards set by other people, such as celebrities, magazines and the media. But you will need the strength of character to resist all of that and we will learn in following chapters how exactly do that.

Most of us don't live minimalistic lifestyles these days. We might think we do to some degree, but we're so easily attracted to physical things and ownership that it takes a real change of mindset to achieve the minimalistic standard. The end result of achieving minimalism is contentment, an easier life and a happier mind.

To sum up, minimalism is:

•Living life with just the things you need

•Asking yourself whether you really need something or you just want it

•An intention and spoken vow that you will not clutter your life with the things that hold no meaning in your life and for your higher self

•Not only about physical goods to own, but also about relationships and friendships in life

•A way to achieve total contentment and happiness

•A mindset and a way of life, not something which can be dibbed in and out of

Why People Practice Minimalism

You might wonder why people bother practising minimalism when there are so many fancy goods to own. Let's face it, it's nice to buy the latest iPhone and have time to sit and play with it, but what you should ask yourself is what value it brings to your life. Sure, it takes great photographs and you can play games on it whenever you please, but does that make you truly happy ? Does it make your life worthwhile ? Does it create a sense of contentment ? Be honest with yourself when trying to find answers to these questions. If you feel in the depths of your soul that upgrading your phone to the next version will bring you lasting happiness then go for it. But it turns out that for most people on this planet, the answer to whether materialistic pursuits bring them lasting happiness is is - Not really, not in the long-run at least.

People choose to practice minimalism because they're fed up of feeling like they're always trying to achieve something and never actually gaining the benefits. For instance, in a short while, we're going to talk about the modern need to always match standards, e.g. Instagram influencers and their power over society. If we're always trying to reach an unspoken standard, e.g. have a certain look, or own a certain type of phone, it's never going to be enough. Why? Because these standards and trends are always changing. Life never stands still. You might have the latest phone for, say, six months. Then a new version comes onto the market and yours is outdated. It's exhausting! You're chasing an ideal that will never be true.

On the other hand, minimalism is not about that constant hamster wheel, you're still, you're static, and you're happy where you are. You have what you need to live your life and you're content. Never underestimate how fantastic being content feels !

People choose to live a minimalistic lifestyle because they no longer want to chase an unrealistic ideal, they don't want to try and 'keep up with the Kardashians' anymore, and they're tired of nothing ever being enough. When you live in a minimalistic way, everything is enough, and that's the whole point.

Another reason why someone might decide to go down the minimalist route is stress. For many of us, the daily life is always so busy and full of running around from one thing to another. It becomes overwhelming, tiring, and depressing. In some cases, you hit a wall, and you can no longer do it. You start to ask yourself if it's all worth it, and you want to make changes - right now. Choosing the minimalist way is the single best way to combat stress and choose a quieter, more peaceful life.

Look at it this way - when you're out with your partner or a close friend, do you become annoyed at them because they always seem to be on their phone? You've come out to eat a meal together and spend quality time, but he or she is messaging someone far away, or checking the latest news online, perhaps scrolling through Instagram. This is such a common occurrence these days. We lose sight of the relationships which are right in front of us, because we're too busy living in a digital world, one that doesn't actually exist. We don't see the beauty of the things around us because we're too busy staring at a small piece of plastic which connects us to what we think is the 'world'. If only the millennials could understand that it's not the world, it's a virtual reality that they're choosing to plug into.

When you choose to be a minimalist, you give yourself the power to open your eyes to the wonder of nature, the beauty all around you, and you can dedicate time to the important relationships in your life. Slow down, smell the daisies!

Origins & Historical References of Minimalist Living

Minimalism has been practised throughout history and actually dates back centuries. Whilst it might not have had a specific name or been a real lifestyle choice, it was simply something which was done in an unspoken manner. Minimalism was much easier back in the day because there weren't as many temptations and certainly not as much emphasis on ownership.

Religious groups in particular, e.g. Buddhists, have long had a history of avoiding or renouncing ownership, in order to become more focused or to gain wisdom. You could even go as far as to think about Buddhist monks or even nuns in the Catholic religion. This is a form of minimalism. Whilst you don't have to go that far if you don't want to, the idea is the same - living with what you need and doing more with it, e.g. gaining wisdom and a more peaceful way of life. You could also adopt the minimalism idea into the Islamic holy month of Ramadan. During this time, Muslims fast during the hours of sunrise to sunset, in order to gain wisdom and a greater sense of clarity. The background idea is the same - you do not need material 'things' in order to gain wisdom or happiness.

Minimalism began to seep its way into the home decoration world sometime in the '70s, becoming trendy to have less in the home, to create a greater space. Again, the idea is the same, even if the type of minimalism we're talking about is more about the mind than the household.

Why Minimalism is so Crucial in The Modern Age

We should point out that minimalism is not about going without. It isn't about denying yourself simple pleasures in life, but it is about reassessing what you consider those pleasure to be. For instance, if you think a simple pleasure is to get a brand new computer, you need to think more critically! Remember, minimalism helps us understand the value of things, so once you have been in this lifestyle for a longer time, you'll begin to see things for what they are and enjoy them for their real value. It's a wonderful feeling to really feel joy in every small thing.

A little earlier we touched upon the modern society's obsessions and why material ownership has run riot. These days, modern culture has decided that happiness lies in owning things, and in having the latest things and more of them. Basically, the more the better, and this somehow equates to power, happiness, and wellness. We are told that happiness lies in the Apple Store or in a shopping mall. Happiness does not lie in either of those places, it lies within you.

We are also always trying to keep up with everyone around us. For instance, if someone you admire owns a new pair of sneakers, you'll be tempted to buy the same ones, because that somehow makes you as good as them. There is nothing bad about you, and you are already as good as them, a pair of sneakers makes no difference! Minimalism, in this case, helps you to become a stronger, more confident person because you're not attempting to compare yourself to others and always seeming to come up short. Consider Instagram influencers for instance - these people are telling us we need to own this product or that product and it will make us beautiful and healthy. Will it really? Deep down we know that person is being paid to market that product and make us believe what they're saying.

Minimalism is so vitally important in the modern day because we are constantly being bombarded with messages via every medium of communication possible. Life isn't about comparisons, it isn't about keeping up with the Jones, the Kardashians, or anyone else. It's about finding value in the smaller things that truly bring us happiness and joy. Escaping the trap of consumerism and daring to seek out happiness and contentment elsewhere can bring huge rewards. Fortune favors the bold. So you should start looking away from your mobile phone or laptop and towards other things (nature, your own experiences, interpersonal relationships etc).

What Will Happen if You Prioritise Materialism Over Minimalism ?

In the long run, if you choose to prioritise materialism over minimalism, you will struggle to be happy. It's that simple. History is full of stories of men and women who chased external entities like gold, empires, power, sex, food, pleasure only to witness the emptiness that faced them on the other side of this pursuit.

You cannot find happiness in something you have purchased. You might feel a rush for a short while, and you might feel pride at owning something so new and shiny, but it will fade and you'll be left with a huge gaping hole once more. This might lead you to try and purchase something else, to get the same rush. Do you see how materialism can lead to addiction for example to shopping?

There is a very real danger for today's generation with addiction and accumulating physical things as opposed to seeking out deeper experiences and meaningful connections.

There are a few outcomes to favouring materialism in your life:

•You will never achieve contentment and happiness

•You will live life in a constant hamster wheel, always trying to reach a goal that is never static, always moving

•You will lack confidence because your self-worth is linked so drastically to ownership

•You run the risk of developing an addiction or dependence on buying new things

•Your financial stability may be at risk as a result

That doesn't paint the greatest pictures, does it? In the upcoming few chapters we will look closer into the root cause of this issue and how we can fix it at the core.

What We Have Learnt in This Chapter

In this chapter, we have learnt what minimalism is and why it is such a beneficial way of life. We have defined it as best as we can and we have talked about why it is so important to become more minimal in our way of thinking in this busy day and age.

Remember, minimalism isn't about never owning anything, and it's not about treating yourself like a slave. Minimalism is about being more aware and questioning whether you really need something versus whether you want it. If you need something in your life, by all means, purchase it. If you just want something, it's time to ask yourself what that product can give you which your relationships and inner happiness can't.

Minimalism is about moving away from consumerism, and about making a choice to avoid materialism. You do not need more 'stuff' to make you happy, and once you realise that you will quickly begin to enjoy a happier, more content life.

This chapter is designed to give you the basics, to help you understand the crux of what we're going to go on and explore in more detail in our upcoming chapters. Make sure you understand the basic points in this chapter that form the basis for the rest of our conversations.

Chapter 8: Setting The Mindset

So how do you get from being that person who has to have the latest iPhone to someone who appreciates that life isn't about possessions? It's not an easy task that lies ahead although the benefits are obvious. Your home will be a haven. You will enjoy life more without the pressures and your family will enjoy the extra time that comes as a direct result of minimalism. How will they gain? Trust me, I asked the same question. If your mind is not racing about how you are going to afford life or whether you can afford Christmas gifts for your kids, you have come to the right place. Your kids have one childhood and that one lacking Christmas present isn't what stays in their minds as they get older. What they want in the here and now are parents who have time to actually enjoy their growing up years and many can't do this because they choose instead to provide the material elements they believe enhance their children's lives and spend more time working than enjoying the families that they have.

If you really want to improve your lot in life, you first need to have the right mindset. This means taking yourself to a place where there is peace and quiet once a day for about 20 minutes – 15 if you can't manage the 20. What I need you to do is empty out the mind so that you get to appreciate what happens when you minimize things. During this twenty minutes a day, I want you to sit on a hard chair and concentrate on your breathing. As you breathe in through your nostrils, count to 7 and then as you breathe out, count to ten. This helps you to stabilize the amount of oxygen that is going through your bloodstream. If you are stressed and unhappy, chances are that you over-oxygenate and this stress will cause you to be more anxious about life. When you do the breathing exercise, try to concentrate on the breathing. Forget about what's going on in the world around you and simply breathe. If you find that thoughts invade your mind, drop them after acknowledging that they are there but learn to give them no importance whatsoever. That means not allowing those thoughts to form chains in your mind. Pull yourself back to concentrating on your breathing.

If you do this first thing in the morning every day before you go to work it has multiple benefits. Even if you have to set your alarm clock early, it's worth it. The habit that you are forming is the habit of mindfulness, which means you are present in those few moments instead of letting your mind wander elsewhere. You may have to force yourself to do this every day, but when you do, you will find that a new habit is forming and that soon you can do this without even thinking about it, just like you do your ablutions or go to the loo every day. It will be just something that you do.

The reason this is important is because it can help you to see clearly the problems that you face in your life. What you are, in effect, doing is closing those cardboard boxes of thought so that you minimize their importance to your life. This helps you to set your mind to the right mindset to tackle all of the clutter in your life. This clear thinking also helps you to get more done within a shorter space of time.

Another thing you can do to enable your mind to concentrate on the act of minimalism is switch off all social media, the phone and the TV when you are not actually concentrating on it. It is an invasion into your life. The sound of the TV, the emotions that come with Internet postings and the interruption in the flow of your thoughts every time an alert goes off on your phone all hold you back from success and enjoyment of life. You don't have to be accountable to other people 24 hours a day. Thus, when it's bedtime, switch off all media in advance so that your mind can slow down and gradually sink into the process of sleep.

A cluttered mind will never help you with the decluttering process because you will always make excuses about why you are keeping some things and getting rid of others. It's really a very simple equation. If the item in question serves no good purpose in your life, then it has to go. Stop doing black and grey and all the shades in between. Start thinking in black and white to make things easier during the decluttering process. Either something adds to your life or it does not. There are no in between items. Yes, there may be things that you are sentimental about, but if these things are meaningful and give you joy then you won't be getting rid of them. It's not a deprivation exercise. It's an exercise in self-restraint, but for a purpose. At this time, your life is muddled because there is too much stuff in it. However, when you have been through the process of minimalizing that stuff, you will be happier and your home will appear to be larger. You will be creating a space at home that is welcoming and warm rather than a reminder that you haven't done enough housework.

As a last exercise, stand outside the main room that you use in the house and close the door. Now, pretend you have never seen that room before and open the door. What's the first thing that you see? I wouldn't mind betting that it won't be something intentionally placed to catch your attention. Instead, it's likely to be the ironing you didn't do last night, the remains of the kids' homework, the coat you didn't hang up yesterday or something that really doesn't have a place in that room. The decluttering process helps you to make every room in your house count. When it's done, you will enter each room of your house and enjoy the focal points that it offers. I promise you that much. I also promise you that the ease it will give to your life is well worth the effort you are about to put in.

Chapter 9: Understand The Essence Of Happiness

Let me tell you next to the concept of love, happiness is probably the most popular concept in American culture. You keep hearing about the concept of happiness. In fact, you keep hearing the word over and over again. It's as if people could all agree that happiness is a top human value. Sounds good so far, right?

The problem is, just like with love, people repeat the word so much that it pretty much has lost its meaning. Don't get me wrong. It does have a meaning; however, the problem is it's confused because people refer to it so much and in so many different contexts. In fact, people mention the word happiness or bring up the concept of happiness when they're trying to sell something to you.

Through this repeated action, we're all left in this confusing fog of concepts. It's no surprise that a lot of people are confused as to what happiness really is because they're getting all these mixed signals from the world. In fact, in many cases, a lot of these signals conflict with each other. Sometimes they cancel each other out.

It's too easy to get lost. It's quite tempting to live your life with a faulty definition of happiness. You end up trying to pursue it but you end up chasing something that's completely different.

This book aims to solve a problem, but just like with any problem-solving initiative, to ensure that we hit the mark, and we achieve what we've set out to accomplish, we need some basic definitions first. It is going to be very difficult to solve a problem if you can't define it properly. In this chapter, we're going to lay a foundation as to what we're trying to achieve so we can then work on taking concrete steps towards it.

Happiness is Not a Product of Your External Circumstances

The first step in personally defining happiness in an effective way for yourself is to understand its sources. It's too easy to think that happiness comes from outside. For example, if you get a promotion, if you meet a very attractive member of the opposite sex who happens to be interested in you, if you were given a gift, so on and so forth. It's easy to think that when any of those situations happen, you are going to be happy, that's what happiness requires. Something happens outside of you.

This is a problem because obviously, we can't control our external circumstances. That's not just going to happen. No matter how hard we try, no matter how many resources we have, up to a certain level, we cannot control our external circumstances.

Now, it doesn't make any sense to base our happiness on things that we can't control, and this is the reason why so many people are unable to achieve happiness because, ultimately, they've defined it as something that has to happen to them. Something has to have the ultimate control. They may take the initiative but, ultimately, it's somebody else's call or the situation has to line up properly, and things have to pan out in a certain way. That's too much to ask for, and that is why a lot of people are unable to achieve real, deep, lasting happiness. It's outside their control. It's beyond their reach.

Happiness is the Effect of Your Internal Assumptions and Expectations

If happiness doesn't ultimately come from outside of us, where does it come from? Well, take the opposite direction. It's you. That's right. Even if you were in a rat cage eating only scraps per day, having to hassle with the oppressive sun, dealing with a tremendous amount of humidity and mosquitoes biting into your skin. Sounds like hell, right?

Well, with the right internal assumptions of expectations, it may not be all that bad.

If you need proof of this, read up Victor Frankl's writings. He was a concentration camp survivor, and he noted that even in the worst conditions, humans, if they take control of how they process reality, can change reality.

So, taking this concept and applying it to practical considerations, it doesn't matter what your external circumstances are. You may be in a pit. You may have gone for several days without food. There might be many physically uncomfortable things going on around you; however, if your mind is right, and you assume certain things and you expect certain things, then you can be very, very happy.

In fact, there are very happy people in developing countries that don't have running water who deal with annual floods, tremendous crime, disease, poverty but their smiles are sincere. They embrace strangers. They're extremely happy to be alive.

Compare this with people who live in the United States who come from median-income households of over $200,000 who are miserable. What's going on? We're not just talking about subjective misery. We're talking about high suicide rates. So, how does this fit?

Well, the explanation should be quite obvious. Happiness is the effect of your internal assumptions and expectations. The good news? You can choose your assumptions and expectations. They are not imposed on you. They're not given to you on a take-it-or-leave-it basis. You can choose them.

Happiness is a Product of Will

The bottom line here is that happiness is a product of your willpower. Pay attention to that word - power. You are more powerful than you give yourself credit for. Your reality may seem like it's set in stone, but it's the reality that you ultimately chose because if you didn't choose it, things will be different. Seriously. Why?

You would make a way. Certain things will be an acceptable, and you would not live with those things. You would think differently which leads to you feeling differently which leads to you behaving differently. Once you start behaving differently, your world starts to change.

It all depends on where you invest your will, and happiness is the product of your will. Whatever level of happiness you have in your life right now, it is a choice. It's not imposed on you. It is a reflection of how you choose to perceive your situation.

Either you could have changed it and did not choose to, or you just chose to look at your present circumstances a certain way. Regardless of how you cut it, you end up with what you have right now. It is ultimately a choice.

The Most Uncomfortable Realization You Would Ever Have

The most inconvenient truth here is that you are always in control. I know, I know.

It doesn't feel like it. You're frustrated to hear that. You may be even shocked. However, you're always in control. Why?

Let's put it this way. In any given day, your body picks up thousands of signals from the outside world. We're talking about things that you can see, hear, touch, taste and smell. We're talking about your sensory inputs.

However, as you probably already know, only a fraction of that are things that you pay attention to. In other words, of all the thousands and thousands of inputs that you perceive every single day, you only manage to notice a fraction. Of that fraction, you only think about or analyze a fraction of that; and of those, you only manage to remember another fraction. Of those memories, only a fraction makes it to your personal narrative or your identity. Do you see how this works?

It might seem like this all takes place on auto pilot, but it doesn't. The things that you choose to perceive are a reflection of your priorities. Certain people who have certain priorities would be more sensitive to certain things. Other people would disregard those and focus on something else.

This process is actually most visible when it comes to interpretation. When you start developing thoughts about the things that you perceive, and you judge them and analyze them, that's when your priorities come into play. That's where your values and prerogatives come into play.

Why is this a big deal? Well, that's how you edit your reality. Editing is all about focusing on certain things and disregarding others. It's all about zooming in on certain details and dismissing others.

Your perception of reality is a reflection of your assumptions and expectations. As a result, your feelings about your world are either corroborated and strengthened, or they are eroded; and you start looking for other assumptions and expectations.

This has a tremendous effect because the way you define reality ultimately is a choice. It really all boils down to what you choose to focus on, how you choose to interpret them, what you leave out and what you let in.

That's a tremendous amount of power and sadly, most people allow themselves to live out desperate and powerless lives trapped in prisons with invisible walls. Imagine walking around feeling trapped, left behind and weak without the understanding that you are holding the key to your mental prison in your hand.

You have the power. Nobody can spring you from your personal prison except yourself, and it all boils down to what you choose to assume and what you choose to expect. It's all about choices.

Chapter 10: Getting Into Minimalism: Simplicity

In many ways, you probably know how to live a simple life, but do you want to? Many people want the complexity and constant drama of their lives. This is something we have to look at honestly. However, some of us really want simplicity, and some would want it if they knew what it felt like to live more simply and at peace.

Just Say No ... Or Say Yes

An important secret to live a simple life is to learn to look honestly at how life gets complicated. This may be different for each of us, but there are some common habits we share. One such habit is taking on new responsibilities without fully acknowledging the costs and complexities they bring to our lives.

When a man buys a boat, for example, does he usually think about the time he will spend maintaining it? Does he think about the trip to the insurance office for insurance, the necessity to shop for accessories like life-jackets and fire extinguishers? Does he remind himself that boats break down, and he will have to deal with hauling it somewhere to have it repaired? Does he consider the trailer-hitch he will need, the tarp to cover the boat, the tarp to replace that one when it tears, the bearings in the trailer wheels that will someday fail. Finally, does he think about the hours he will be committed to working to pay for all this joy?

It is not about the boat, by the way. There is nothing wrong with owning a boat. With nothing else was going on in his life, all of the above could easily be a part of "the simple life." However, when we do not honestly recognize the role of our own choices in adding complexity to us, we take on more than we can possibly handle. As a result, a million exercise equipment are kept unused in basements while ten million hours are spent working to pay for them. Look honestly at all the costs, and make well-informed choices - this is the first secret of how to live a simple life.

Money Brings Simplicity - Or Complexity

Isn't it simple for a rich man to own a boat? He can just pay someone to take care of it while he plays with his children. Money can bring simplicity to your life, but it is all in how you use it. This is the next important secret of how to live a simple life.

People use money in ways that overly complicate life, as when they put a down payment on a hot tub that they really do not need. Then they have to work to pay the interest, they have to clean the bathtub, find a place for it, and have it repaired. Of course, if you are rich enough, someone will take care of these things for you. However, if you make $10 per hour, a hot tub will almost overly complicate your life.

If you really want the simple life, the choice then is to make more money, or live a life that is simply supported by your current income. After I paid off the mortgage loan on my first home, and got rid of the car, life became simpler and free. As I make more money, I can easily add more stuff back into my life, while keeping it simple, as long as I maintain the right balance.

Drama Adds Complexity

For a simpler life, have fewer friends. This may sound harsh, but how many friends do you really need? Don't get rid of true supportive friends, but don't add people to your life unless there is a real exchange of value between you. We all have acquaintances we call "friends" and yet only tolerate just to "be nice." Do you think it is selfish to say you do not owe anything to them? Then how selfish is it for them to say you do?

With friends and family, do not get involved in the drama more than you need to. Watch closely, and you will see that until a person is ready to change, you rarely can help them in any case, neither with words nor with money. Save your efforts for when you truly can help. You were not born with an obligation to anyone, and it is incredibly selfish for anyone to make such claims on your life. Let the drama swirl around you, but do not get involved in it. This is a crucial lesson on how to live a simple life.

Two Pillars for Great and Simple Life

I have spoken to a number of people who want to know 'what life is all about'.

A number of years ago, I had my own questions on this subject. Since then I have listened too and read the theories of people who seemed wise enough.

I think one of the wisest thoughts on the subject came from Woody Allen, He said, 'I'm astounded by people who want to know the universe when it's hard enough to find your way around Chinatown.'

Allen's quote simplifies it for me. We can spend too long looking at the big picture and forget about the smaller picture - our own life.

Our own life is where most of can make the most difference. Sometimes though it is knowing where and what to begin with.

I have become a great believer in people gaining personal clarity. In my opinion, clarity is the number one issue we need to resolve before taking on anything.

I know some people argue for an easier flowing attitude that allows - and at times I would agree this can have huge benefits - However, too much 'what-ever will be, will be,' will mean the ship will just drift. The result being, never building much that is worthwhile.

In coaching sessions I see clients pulling together the lose strands of opportunity and developing them with clarity into something that can make a change, both in their life, their communities and in some cases further afield.

When we understand the first pillar - clarity - the second pillar fits easily into place.

In business if we know we need customers, but do not know whether to sell massage and have a perception that what we offer is for everyone, and then we will have a hard time attracting enough custom to pay your bills.

If however we decide what we most want to do is find massage clients, then define the section of the population that have a need for our service, we have not just found clarity, but the meaning to pursue a significant number of people who could help us provide a service they need. This is much more fruitful that the what-ever will be.

If we feel fed up with life and think that more TV or a holiday in sun is the answer, we will struggle to find what we need. If we read, go on workshops and speak with other seekers, we will turn the inspirational thought - that there must be more in life into a reality.

So while the first pillar is clarity, the second is meaning. Clarity hones in. Meaning, creates the drive. Here is an example of how I put everything in this newsletter into something that works.

In life, years ago, I knew I wanted to create something better. At first, I did not know what that was and I read hundreds of books went on all kinds of workshops and met many people, until it became clearer to me, what I wanted my life to be about.

Having decided what I wanted, I had the meaning to engage other people into my dreams. Where our dreams matched, magic happened, and still does.

You will find some useful tips below...

1. Understand it is okay to drift sometimes.

2. Keep an eye out for moments of inspiration that can shape your future reality

3. As things take shape, start to work out how you can help the process, create clarity.

4. Write your clarity down. Make it 1-2 sentences.

5. With clarity meaning will follow and you will find like-minded people easier to engage on your mission.

Chapter 11: Being Minimalistic

Minimalism originates from the art and design world. If you have ever experienced yourself wondering about any canvas in a museum, which is painted in one color, then it is 'less is more aesthetic.' Minimalism here is used to describe the perspective of our thoughts, possessions, and our lives. It has a different meaning for different people. Certain connotations from the world of art and design can help you understand minimalism better though it is not the context of this book. For instance, to some, white spaces, clean lines, less is more, are considered by some minimalism. It is a conventional description, which does not apply to everyone when considering what their home should look like or what they want their life to be about. Therefore, from this context, it is finding joy in simplicity and what makes you content and nothing more.

What Minimalism Is

- Letting go of anything that is of no use

- A life based on how you want to live and not about other's expectations

- Eliminating obsessive and negative thoughts

- Reflection of yourself in the space around your living space

- Surrounding yourself with textures and colors that make you feel better

- Laying furniture in a way that defines how you live instead of how others live

- Finding more than one purpose for an object

- Knowing what you have is enough

- Spending on adventures and experiences

What Minimalism Is Not?

- Agreeing to every request

- Maintain things out of obligation or loyalty to someone

- Making sure your life is straight out of a décor magazine

- Giving everything up

- About organizing your possessions

Consumer Cultures

The accumulation of material possessions does not help you find yourself. Everyone is aware of this, but we still accumulate possessions to find happiness. But the fact is, real happiness comes from within us – it is a result of who we are. Similarly, discontent is also because of the person we have become. So, if you live with intentions and meaning you will be happy, satisfied, and fulfilled most of your life. If you aspire to live like the average person, this book would be of no help because the average person is not happy. You do not have to settle for mediocrity, just for the sake of it or because people around you are settling for it.

Associating and being influenced by our culture is normal and acceptable - except when the cultural attitude is detrimental. Consumerism is one of those factors that is hugely damaging. We consume and create for our enjoyment and use, which are considered essential. Since these things do not last forever, we create more. Therefore, we have always been consumers, and we will remain consumers. However, this concept should be examined.

During the 1930s and '40s, World War II and The Great Depression made it difficult to lead a consumer-based lifestyle. Everything was handmade, rarely store bought, and in such cases, it was always maintained and repaired. These cautious measures were a necessity and a patriotic duty because of the war. After the war, America entered an economic and political culture based on mass consumption. It was criticized by Lizabeth Cohen saying that this cultural ideology of consumption as a patriotic act is a product of political jargon of post-war America with profound and far-reaching impacts. This American dream of buying more and more is still relevant today, promoted by the advertising industry. Today's advertising has become a vital tool in the shaping of the collective American and global consciousness.

The television ad industry was built over time as a platform for selling advertisement spaces. The broadcasts are timed by the number of viewers that watch each show. Advertisers pay millions to make sure that their product is seen alongside a popular show. These commercials are incredibly influential, and that makes them invest with no bounds. This influence starts right after we are born. The message that each advertisement carries is not −buy our product− but they try to convince you that you will be happier, cooler, and thinner if you acquire that product. It makes your entire life look flawless. The message focuses on your identity and to change your perspective on how your life should be lived. We become so unaware of these manipulations and mind games that we forget that they affect us. Think about clothes, when we purchase them; with brand names ornamented on them. It is free advertising - advertising that we pay for by buying from them and being walking billboards. It proves that people aren't just buying for quality or even beauty of the clothes, but to be associated with a specific form of sensibility, elegance, sex appeal, or an adventurous spirit. The brand you choose fits you into a self-identity that you desire. These associations are immensely promoted by brands through advertisements.

Marketing manufactures promote needs that an average person doesn't require. This phenomenon is not just limited to the U.S. In Europe, a marketing campaign for a feminine wash tells women that their intimate areas can get fairer when using their product, and apparently, it is gynecologist recommended. It is evident here that most women would never consider that they need a change in color of their private parts, owing to health risks until they see these advertisements.

Advertisements in any form are illusions. Most times they are artistically created and beautiful, that we can enjoy like a good movie. Our subconscious will not be able to realize that they are illusions. We forget that there is an entire team of producers and directors behind these commercials. As a result, once we go shopping, we end up purchasing something that we didn't even know we needed. Even buying from luxury stores or a superstore, enhances our experience. They affect our buying habits.

As it turns out, we are the captains of our ship. It demands an emphasis on effort and intentional living to resist the consumer culture we thrive in and pursue a life in a way that we deeply desire. Living a minimal life has been in and off vogue over the years, and it has been referred to as downsizing, decluttering, simpler living, and recently, minimalism.

Minimalism is about what it provides, not what it cuts off. It is an intentional focus on things that has the most value and disregard for anything that diverts us from them. Minimalism fills us with hope. With this perspective in mind, let us clear up some commonly stated misconceptions about minimalism.

Misconception 1

It is about giving up everything

Certain people tend to believe that minimizing means discarding everything or almost everything. That is not it, in most cases. It is rather about living with less and not about living with nothing. When you walk into your home, you mostly would not consider it as a minimalistic family home. In your living room, there would be seating for six, framed photographs, rugs, a coffee table, and a television. You might find coat closets with baseball caps, jackets and winter clothes. In your children's room, there might be craft supplies, books, and toys. We look forward to living minimally, but at the same time, we are still breathing, living, and changing. To survive is to consume. So, we do have possessions. However, we work hard to get away from the excessive accumulation of worldly possessions. It is humanly impossible to get rid of everything. Instead, people need to get rid of things that are unnecessary to pursue their goals in life.

Be passionate about your soul, about loving and influencing others, and also about your family. Focus on prioritizing this above everything else. Minimalism helps remove physical hindrances so that you can easily prioritize. It helps to ruthlessly get away from things that are not true to your goals. At the same time if there are things you need to live a certain life and enjoy, keep them, and do not feel guilty. Do not make the mistake of imagining that you have to live with nothing. Take what gives you the life you want.

Misconception 2

It is about organizing

Organizing does have a place here, but it's not the same as minimizing. Organizing is a temporary solution that we have to repeat over time. If organizing had worked, it would have been done by now. In the simplest sense, organizing is rearranging. Even though we have storage solutions, there will be new ones tomorrow, which will be forced on us. Organizing also has some shortcomings:

It doesn't benefit anyone else

These items we organize sit on shelves in our attics and garages with no benefit to anyone even if it's of use to others.

IT DOESN'T solve your problems with money

It doesn't put an end to the core spending problems. The act of rearranging costs us more since we purchase containers, larger homes with storage units, etc.

IT DOESN't solve our "desire" to have more

Organizing things into plastic bins, extra closets, or boxes is about holding excessive accumulation. This draws us to go after the culturally driven definition of happiness.

It doesn't force us to "evaluate" our life

Even though reorganizing helps to assess what we own, it doesn't allow us to ask ourselves if we need it all. Most often we put them back into cartons and forget about them.

It doesn't "accomplish" much to make way for change

It might garner a temporary uplifted feeling, but it rarely leads to a lifestyle change. We will still consider our house small, our income still insufficient and not enough time in a day. We end up rearranging our possessions but never our lives.

Contrarily, the act of discarding possessions can help accomplish your purpose. It is a permanent solution, which will stay for good. Organizing is better than doing nothing, but minimizing is far better than that.

Your choice, your purpose

The ultimate advantage of minimalism is that it helps you be in a track that focuses on your passions. However, there is more to it; it reveals a sense of clarity to what those passions are. Take a leap of faith and shape your expression of minimalism. It's a goal-directed by the need to unburden our life, which helps us accomplish more.

Ultimately your practice of a minimalistic lifestyle is going to be different from what others have. You might live on a farm or have a small family or no family. You might love sports, movies, music, and books. Maybe you believe that your purpose is to host the most beautiful dinner parties and retreat for others.

Follow your passions with the ability and resources you own. Discard your distractions and fulfill your passions and find a style of minimalism that works for you. One that is functional but liberating. Also, be aware that your understanding of minimalism doesn't happen overnight. It will take time to evolve, and it will change you dramatically.

It will require give and take. You can expect mistakes along the journey. Therefore, this path will also teach you humility.

Where to start

Mark Twain said, "The two most important days of our life are the day that we are born and the day that we find out why."

In our opinion, the third most important day is the day that you get rid of any distractions that are holding you back from pursuing your purpose.

Once your approach towards simplifying your life becomes individualized, it is easier to win. It makes you feel more comfortable. You will sustain it, which frees you up to express yourself and lead you to be what you were meant to be. How do we accomplish this?

To clarify your own goals, you should start by examining yourself. Get a grip on your abilities, weaknesses, and talents, also the issues that get you angry. To help with this, grab a piece of paper and write out your answers to the following questions.

What moments both good and bad, have shaped your life?

What are the similarities that are most common in your accomplishments?

What problems are you most passionate about solving?

What line of work would you be drawn to if it weren't for money issues?

Which passion do you most regret not following?

What is the legacy that you want to leave?

Whom do you most look up to in life? Specify characteristics that you want to emulate.

Continue to expand on these questions as you read the book. The ultimate theme of your goal will become increasingly important in the following chapters. However, from now on, it is essential to realize that your purpose is not to live someone else's life. So, determine what the best possible version of yourself would be through minimalism that works for you.

Chapter 12: How To Declutter The Mind

There are lots of tricks and tips you can use to declutter your mind. But you must discover what is best for you and the area of your soul you want to declutter. In this chapter, we will look at some of the best tricks you can use to declutter your mind.

Keep a Priority List

We all know the importance of to-do lists. But the problem with most of these is that they are cluttered. This is where priority lists come in. They show a limited number of activities that are most important. Ideally, this list should only have 2–4 items.

In the book the Organized Mind, Daniel Levitin argues that the mind can only focus on 3–4 things at a time. Any more than this stresses it. And lots of studies show that long to do lists are really a sure-fire way to stress your mind.

So I recommend having a priority list and not just a simple schedule. If you find you can't trim your list, then automate some tasks. If you cannot automate, then hire others to help you. Of course, you will first need to ensure that the tasks are only essential ones. Otherwise, follow the guide in the last chapter.

Also, you must ensure that you keep your tasks on a single sheet of paper. This will make accessing them less taxing for your brain. And having a paper means you don't have to remember that you have a priority list somewhere – a paper can be kept beside your desk. No need to open applications, input passwords, etc.

Empty it on Paper

Writing things on paper comes with lots of benefits. Among them is that as you write, you literally empty your clutter onto the paper. Lots of studies show that this gets negative emotions off your mind. For instance, a Stanford study showed that writing things down allows you to adopt a healthier attitude and reduce your stress levels.

Paper is like your junk box or trash can. So whether it is negative emotions, tasks, ideas, or what have you, write it down.

Let Go

Are you still holding on to past hurts, grudges, or painful experiences? You need to let all these go. The problem with keeping negative feelings is that you relive them. And if it is pain in question, you get to experience the pain all over again. If it is anger, you also get to feel the anger again.

Basically, not letting go of negative feelings translates into giving those feelings freedom to live in your mind.

Thankfully, there is an easy solution to this. First, you'll have to make a conscious decision that you are going to let go. And then you must let go.

Another trick is to write the painful thing down. If it is a grudge, write a letter to the person who hurt you telling them you have forgiven them. You might send the letter if you want, but it is just as well to tear it. Writing the feeling down lets you confront it.

A third trick is to focus on other areas of the feeling. For instance, if you are thinking of a painful thing someone did to you, just focus on other good things related to the incident. You can think of a friend who comforted you during this tough time. The Beckman Institute of Art at the University of Illinois found that this alone can make you forget negative feelings and realize that all is not dark.

Limit the Garbage

There is no point in cleaning a room if you will keep adding garbage into it. The same is true for your soul. You need to stop bringing trash into it. This will lessen the need and amount of decluttering that you will have to do later.

You must limit your time on TV, radio, social media, magazines, etc. All these promote consumerist behavior.

Do What You Can Now

If you always put aside little decisions for later, then you may be cluttering your brain unnecessarily. When you put off making a decision or doing a simple task, you create a mental note of that thing. And the more such tasks you put aside, the more clutter you will have in your brain. So learn to make decisions promptly if you can.

For decisions or tasks that won't take more than 2 minutes, do them right away. You will free your mental resources.

Sleep

Most of us do not get enough sleep. And we go about boasting about this as if it is an admirable thing. Getting enough sleep is important for all of us. A good night's rest refreshes the mind. And research exists to show that sleep really does clear the head.

Ideally, you must sleep for at least 7 hours every day. But you must never let this exceed 8 hours.

Also, the quality of your sleep matters. Make sure your room is set to the right temperature, considered to be 60 to 67 degrees Fahrenheit. The lights must be turned off or you may use a sleeping mask. To make falling asleep easier, go to bed at the same time every day. In addition, don't drink a lot of water just before bed to avoid waking up constantly.

Connect with Nature

Being in touch with nature has healing effects. It soothes your soul and calms your speeding mind down. You learn to appreciate that you do not need luxury things to experience the beauty of life.

The problem is that most of us have lost touch with nature. We are so busy with man-made stuff that we find it impossible to appreciate the free wonders of the world.

Go walk in forests. Go sit beside a river. Go climb a hill.

Don't Multitask

If you are fond of multitasking, then you are hurting yourself. Multitasking fills your head with a lot of work and mental notes. And that clutters your soul and makes you feel stressed.

Instead, learn to do one thing at a time. You will feel much less exhausted if you do that. You will be happy and healthy.

Chapter 13: An Ideal Way To Stop Spending And Start Living

Modernization has shifted our focus from living to spending. It is the age where you have the latest gadgets but do not use even 10% of them. You have wardrobes full of clothes but haven't tried 80% of the clothes for months and aren't even planning to do so. Your home is full of items that you do not use but you have bought anyhow.

These items do not come for free. They have a cost and you had to spend your days and nights earning to buy these things. It was a time that wouldn't come back. Effectively, you have spent that chunk of time on things that are futile. You could have made better use of that time. You could have learned something new if you weren't busy with earning to buy those things. You could have traveled in that time and seen new places and known new people. You could have spent that time with your loved ones who feel ignored and complain about lack of time and attention. You could have spent that time on self-improvement. You could have spent that time helping others in need. However, you choose to spend that time in slogging your hours to buy the items that are giving you no pleasure at all.

This is like living with a herd mentality. You give away your chance to live consciously to follow trends. These trends change much faster than your anticipation and you get busy in earning for the new trend. It is a vicious cycle that would never end if you don't choose to live consciously. Minimalism is the way to do that.

It helps you in understanding your needs and minimizing them so that you can focus on more important things in life. It is a way to add more value to your life.

Being a minimalist doesn't mean giving away all joys of life. On the contrary, it is about enjoying life more keenly. When you start living consciously, you have more time to focus on things of importance. You are not swayed by worthless advertisements. Midnight sales stop exciting you as you already have the things that you need. You can treat yourself with the best in class things as you know that you are going to put them to full use. Your financial stress goes down as you are spending less on useless things. You have more time for yourself.

Time is the single most important thing that you cannot afford to lose. Money or material objects hold no importance in front of time. It is unidirectional and would never go back. The time you lose is gone. Minimalism helps you in making full use of this time. You can focus all your energies on using this time to your advantage. You can gain knowledge and experience at this time as these are the only thing that lasts. They are valued irrespective of your class or social status.

We are wasting a lot of time watching the last-minute sales and not focusing on the smile of our kids. We are letting our loved ones feel lonely while we are busy earning just for buying things. This must stop. Minimalism gives you the chance to make conscious decisions on buying things or keeping things in your life.

You get a chance to decide your priorities and life and focus on them. It is a chance much more important than getting any prized item produced till date. So, stop living to buy things and start focusing on living this life to the fullest.

Chapter 14: The 15-Minute Rule

Who has not dedicated a whole Saturday to doing the home cleaning? It is exhausting, it becomes an ordeal and the worse thing ... it doesn't work. We have the solution; do it bit by bit. Start by dividing your home into zones and establish new routines.

So, if you dedicate 15 minutes every day (yes, only 15 minutes!), you will not dread when the weekend approached as it is no longer necessary to do it all at once and you can dedicate your time to everything, except clean up. And forget about the dreaded cleaning marathons!

Day 1: Start in the morning

Duration: 5 minutes

Attempt to "clean up" as much as possible before you leave home in the morning.

Make the bed. Hang your towels after your shower. Place your mug in the kitchen's sink or in the dishwasher.

These are habits. Form your own important 2-4 habits and see what a difference it makes to your life.

Without forgetting about the night

Duration: 10 minutes

This is the time of the night that you want to switch off. But wait! Make it a nightly routine to do a quick "sweep of your home." Pick up that teddy lying on the floor. The bath towel from the morning, pick it up and place it on the rack, etc. The key to the success of this method is to never skip the nightly routine. It is a commitment that will allow you to start the next day on the right foot.

Key point: Focus on the kitchen

Leave it clean and in order. Pick up the table, put the dishwasher, scrub all the utensils and leave the countertop clear. You will appreciate it in the morning when you are preparing breakfast in a clean and orderly kitchen.

Note: That task is not the same as the others because it is the only continuous task. Perhaps, you will have to do it every day to keep the kitchen clean and your bed made. But if you follow that daily routine, you will have those spaces in order.

Day 2: Choose a moment in a day to unravel

Duration: 15 minutes

An organized home is also one that is not full of objects that you don't like or use. Also, you want space. Your first mission is to identify the "junk," that is, things that you have not used for more than a year objects that you have been given and don't like; clothes that have become too small or maybe too big.

When I do it?

Don't wait for the change of season; you'll be overwhelmed enough with the change of wardrobe. Take advantage of 15 minutes of your daily area to find them.

Pay attention, and you can quickly fill a bag.

Day 3: All in one go: drying, folding and storing clothes

Duration: 15 minutes

To be able to say goodbye to each one of the mountains of clothes to wash, to iron, to keep, etc., every day that is necessary you must start the washing machine routine in the morning. And then, whether you use a dryer or dry the clothes outdoors or indoors, once it's dry, do all the steps in one go. Avoid folding the clothes later as you can be sure of a pile-up in no time.

Well saved

Choose a time of the day when you can finish the whole process: Iron (if you do), fold and save. If you don't have time to iron, plan a fixed space to place the clothes.

Day 4: Attack the chaos room

Duration: 5 minutes a day (three days)

It's the typical room you go to for everything you don't know where to keep or don't have a fixed place for. And it's that door that you always close when you have guests. That room is in a cluttered state, and you cannot be bothered to organize it because you don't know where to start.

The solution? Do it little by little

Start a 5 minute a day routine. Yes, just five minutes. At first, you will not notice the difference, but after a few days, that room will begin to feel purposeful and useful. Do not fall into the trap of cluttering the room again.

Day 5: Express cleaning: focus on the living room and bathroom

Duration: 15 minutes

Having visitors at home is great, but when they show up unexpectedly, they can cause a bit of stress. Don't worry, your home will look perfect if you go over the kitchen and you focus on the living room and the bathroom. Pick up everything that is out of place in the room. Fluff up the sofa cushions and clear the coffee table. In the bathroom, clean the toilets and place fresh towels.

The weekend is coming?

A little review and a lot of rest: Invest a few minutes on Friday or the weekend to get a bit of cleaning done. It should not take more than an hour to sweep and scrub the living room, kitchen, and bathroom. Take the opportunity to change the towels and sheets of the beds and empty bins. And then, sit back and enjoy.

Tips:

Plan your needs well and, if your agenda is at its peak, allocate each day to only one activity. The dreaded Monday is usually the best time to organize the week in general, make the shopping list (better if you think about the menus before), review the agenda, etc. On Tuesday, buy fresh produce, and Wednesday is a perfect day to check papers and bills.

The errands, if there is no urgency, leave them for Thursday. Go to the cleaners, to the greengrocer. On Friday, you can lower the pace a little as the weekend kicks in, which is when you should take advantage to enjoy your deserved rest.

Chapter 15: Mental Minimalism: Let Go And Be Free

I understand that chapter two involves a lot of wrestling with your preconceived ideas and thing that you have seen to be true about yourself. To be completely honest with you, chapter two is where all the action takes place. Get that right and everything else pretty much flows from it.

In this chapter, we're going to go from your mindset. We're going to go into your mental habits and regular emotional states. You can also choose to practice minimalism on this level.

Different Perceptions of Minimalism

Please understand that there are many different people practicing minimalism, and they have many different methods and different objectives. Some people focus primarily on cutting out the physical clutter, so they let go of a large chunk of their material possessions. Many move into tiny houses or smaller living quarters, others give up on sedentary living all together and they travel from place to place.

This also applies to their work. Instead of showing up at the same place, working nine to five and waiting for a paycheck every two weeks, they become freelancers, or they operate online businesses that enable them to earn a passive income. So, they're able to travel all over the world while the checks regularly come in.

Passive income, after all, it doesn't involve you agonizing over every dollar you earn. You set up websites, and when people visit those websites click on ads, buy stuff or do whatever it is that you get paid for, you make money. So, you just check your PayPal account and you get all these payments from your many different passive income projects.

There is a wide range of variations to this. You can freelance, so this means you're selling your time and skills, or you can set up passive income websites. You can also dropship, so basically, you're setting up a front end for a Chinese or overseas vendor.

When somebody visits your website and pays for something, you set up a software that automatically turns around and orders from your supplier, and your supplier bypasses you directly. They ship directly to your customer.

There are so many variations to this. You can also publish a book like this and put it up on Amazon Kindle and forget about it. When people buy, you earn a royalty, and enough time passes, you get a royalty check from Amazon courtesy of their Kindle Self-Publishing Program.

There are many levels to minimalism, but none of those levels would really have much value if they don't also lead to some form and some level of mental minimalism. Put in a nutshell, mental minimalism is really all about letting go and being truly free.

Sounds awesome, right? In fact, you've probably read all sorts of online sales pages talking about the same stuff, but usually, they talk about this in the context of financial freedom. But the truth is, practicing minimalism can help you let go of worry and fear.

It can help you truly live instead of chasing a paycheck or allowing financial worries to rob your joy. Here is just a framework on how this can happen.

Background: The Prison of Worry and Fear

As the famous French Enlightenment Philosopher Jean-Jacques Rousseau, famously said: "Man is born free, but everywhere he is in chains."

While Rousseau made this statement in terms of political philosophy, it is nonetheless true on a practical level. People walk around in mental prisons. You can't see the four walls. It's not made out of cement or concrete. There're no iron bars or any kind of physical obstacle, but they're prisoners nonetheless.

Do you have things that you're guilty about? Do you have things that you regret, that you wish you would have done? Well, if that's the case, you're living in a prison of the past. These are the things that you wish you could learn or you feel that you could have done it, you should have done it. But the past is past. It's already happened. That ship has already sailed.

The bottom line is you can't undo those facts. Maybe you're another kind of mental prisoner. Maybe you're constantly anxious about things that are about to pop off, that there seems to be a disaster in the making just around the corner. Well, what you're really fearful of is the future. You're worrying yourself about things that have yet to happen. This too is a waste of time, just as agonizing over the past.

The problem is when we allow the past or the anxiety of the future get to us, we suffer in the present. Worse yet, we lay out the foundation for a crappy future. This is the prison that a lot of people are in. Now some have it worse than others, but this is the reality that we constantly contend with.

This is real because the sense of disappointment, frustration and the gnawing realization about living far below our fullest potential robs joy. We're not quite there. The happy moments aren't as bright. There's always this emotional "stuff" cluttering our minds and our feelings.

To get out from under this, mental minimalism employs a few principles.

Focus On What You Can Control

What can you control? Be honest with yourself. Can you control the past? Can you, like Marty McFly get into a souped-up DeLorean and set a preset time schedule and go back to the past? Of course not. The time machine is yet to be invented, so the facts will remain exactly that, facts. There's nothing you can do about them.

You can feel lousy about them, but guess what? It doesn't matter how bad you feel; those facts are going to remain the same. What can you do? Let go. How? Realize that these are fact. They've already happened. There's nothing you can do about them.

So, you accept it and you learn to forgive. Maybe somebody traumatized you in the past. Maybe they did something horrible to you. Maybe you did something bad to somebody else. Learn to forgive. Forgive yourself, forgive the other person.

I know this sounds crass, but one of the most selfish and self-serving things you could do is to forgive. I know it boggles the mind because a lot of people would say, "Well, am I not compromising myself? Am I not losing out?" No. You're taking care of yourself when you do that because the number one beneficiary of forgiveness is you.

You think you're hurting those people by continuing to agonize about how the cheated you or left you behind, or made you lose out, or in whatever way, shape or form harmed you? Of course, not They've moved on. In fact, they're probably very happy right now. So, who exactly are you hurting agonizing over the past?

Forgive and forgive again and again, until it takes. It's not easy. This is not how human beings are wired but this is precisely what you need to do. You have to overcome that. When you let go past hurts, you start to rediscover what it's like to love and respect yourself.

Respect yourself enough to let go. A lot of people have false pride. They think that the highest form of giving themselves the respect that they are due is to never let go and never forget and never forgive. Well, here's the problem. As I have mentioned above, who does that hurt? Not the perpetrator.

147

The person who harmed you is gone. Maybe they're dead. Maybe they've gone on harming other people or more likely than not, they've changed. So even if you were given an opportunity to confront that person and say to that person, "You're a horrible person! You did this to me!" Your words will ring hollow and you would know it. Why? You're talking to a changed person.

Maybe he or she was immature or was in a very tough spot, or was really crying within when they did those things. They were lashing out precisely because they were hurting so deeply. What happens then? So, learn to forgive because you're doing it for yourself, and you're declaring independence from the trauma of that memory.

It no longer has a hold on you. Understand and celebrate your personal circle of emotional competence, and it begins with forgiveness. It begins with developing a healthy relationship with the past. Here's a spoiler: None of us have a perfect past.

There are very few people (and I even doubt that) who have perfect lives where everything is happy. There will always be trauma. So, allow yourself to start building emotional competence in the here and now. One crucial way to do that is to learn to develop a healthy relationship with your past, and this means forgive, learn and forget the facts.

Hang on to the lesson but forget the facts because a lot of people say, "Well I can forgive, but I'll never forget." Well, that's a problem because when you refuse to forget, the old feelings come back. You only need the wrong trigger and you're back to square one.

None of this is to say that you should not learn. I would say that that's absolutely crucial. But you can learn, forgive and forget the operative facts. Hang on to the lesson and move on. This is how you practice power over what you can control.

You can't control those people and you can't control the past. You can't control those facts. You can't control how you continue to respond to what happened. This is how you build emotional competence because you keep tightening that control and get stronger and stronger until you become an emotionally strong person.

This leads to resilience, and guess what? Victory in the future.

Let Go of Worry and Fear

By focusing on what you can control, you become responsible for what you're consciously building inside. This means you start developing real confidence. Believe it or not, people who spend a ridiculous amount of their time worried and fearful are not all that confident.

In fact, they're operating so far away from real confidence. How can they? They're simply reacting. They're not in control. So, when certain things happen, they get triggered, they can't help it. So, they're back to square one. Be responsible for what you're consciously building inside.

This is crucial to mental and emotional competence. This is crucial to you picking and choosing the character that you're growing into. This ability to choose and this ability to take action on it is not philosophical. This is not academic nor theoretical. This is real because you base real confidence on that.

And the best part is that it is happening in the here and now. This will only grow when you take action on it now, and the way to do it is focusing on your control and letting go of worry and fear. Sadly, too many of us allow ourselves to be simply bent out of shape by focusing on what could be or should be. And when we look at how our lives are playing out, we're unhappy.

Too many of us are constantly saying to ourselves this is not how things should be. Welcome to the club. Maybe the better approach would be to look at how things are instead of how you wish they could be or they should be. When you do this and focus on the here and now, and focus on what you can control by forgiving and establishing a better relationship with not only the past but current reality, you become free.

You're no longer driven by fantasies of the past or unrealistic expectations of the future. Most importantly, you're no longer dependent on other people. If you're completely honest with yourself, and you allow yourself to agonize over the past, you're basically just waiting for that person to say "I'm sorry."

You're waiting for somebody to make amends. You're waiting for this and that and the other, but they can all be boiled down to somebody taking some sort of action so you can feel good about yourself. Do you see how ridiculous that is?

Do you see how powerless you have made yourself to be? You deserve more. You're more than that so focus on what you can control now and pull that trigger. Base your confidence and well-being on the here and now. Base it on reality that you can control.

Quit waiting because you'll be waiting forever.

Stop Sabotaging Yourself with the Past or Future

I used to do this a lot. I would be struggling financially and I would say, "Well, in the future maybe I could invent something or I can get this amazing job, and in an instant, my worries and problems disappear."

I remained in that mental state for a while, and then once things wear off, I'm back to where I began, still stressed. Still wondering when the next dollar is going to come from. Pretty sad, right? Welcome to daydreaming.

Believe it or not, this activity that we thought we outgrew in junior high quickly becomes an adult habit. When you're fantasizing or daydreaming of resolving the past or achieving some sort of result in the future, what you're really doing is you're walking in chewing gum.

I know that sounds ridiculous, but that's exactly what you're doing. You're putting yourself in a mental state that is so far removed from where you are, but at the same time using the emotional rush created by this to deal with the stress you're feeling with the here and now.

I'm sorry to be the one to break this to you, but if you have a problem now, resolve it now. All the warm, fuzzy and hopeful feelings you get fantasizing and daydreaming is not going to do you a lick of good, because that bill, that credit card payment, that mortgage, that failing relationship and everything else needs to be handled now.

Not tomorrow, not the day after. Now.

This is why it's really important to stop waiting. Forgive, resolve, let go and move on. Not tomorrow. Now. let go of daydreaming. Consistently interrupt yourself and say, "I'm going to get rid of this mental clutter. This is worthless."

This just produces emotional clutter that functions like some sort of neurotransmitter candy. I feel hopeful but I'm nowhere closer to the solution because I've robbed myself of the solution. Please understand that when you're feeling heat and pressure because of stuff that you need to pay, or problems that you're confronting, you have to step up, and that means stop fantasizing, stop waiting for somebody to come up with the answer and do it yourself.

Stop daydreaming about quick solutions to current problems. You're just mentally and emotionally escaping. Deal with your issues today. And the good news is, no matter how big the problem is, it can usually be broken down, so start with those small solutions.

Now, a lot of this won't be perfect. I mean, let's face it, a lot of us would want to somehow, someway wave some sort of magic wand to make our personal challenges go away, but that's not going to happen. Not even close. So, break down whatever issues that you're dealing with today into smaller, easier to manage parts and get to it.

You can't wait. Waiting will just make things worse. This is how you get rid of emotional and mental clutter.

Chapter 16: Create Room For Things Which Are Important And Which Deserve It

In order to be successful with the implementation of minimalistic principles, it is necessary to really think about what you want to achieve in your life and what kind of home design has to be achieved to make sure that your goals are achieved.

You don't want to be in a situation where your home is an obstacle to working toward your goals and to working effectively and efficiently. It should be the opposite, your home is what should make things easier for you so that you have a better chance of accomplishing what you want.

The question you may be asking now is why does it happen that so many people don't utilize this philosophy of home and life design? The answer to that is actually quite simple and it boils down to the fact that some people simply don't know what they want from their home and from life as a whole. One thing that could be blamed for all this is media and marketing since they are constantly showing us a supposedly better way to live which is better than what we are currently doing. This makes it hard to be satisfied and to know what you actually want. As a consequence, it is easy to get lost in a sea of different marketing agendas and goals. It is really hard to be truly happy when we are constantly hearing about a better way to do something.

In order to not fall for anything, you need to stand for something. You need to sit down and to really think about what is important to you and what you want to get out of life since you can't get what you want if you don't know what you want. You should write down an affirmation based on what you want and you can start to build your ideal home by using that as a guide. The point is that you don't want to be without the knowledge of what goals are important and the strategies for moving towards those goals.

Turn Your Home Into Your Ally

Maybe you came to the realization that what you really value the most in your life are the people close to your and music. Now that you have this knowledge, you can start designing your Home appropriately. For example, you may design your home in a way that accommodates guests so that they want to spend more time there. The rooms which would go a long way towards accomplishing these design goals would be some form of entertainment rooms such as rooms with comfy furniture and a large television accompanied with a large table for all the snacks. As far as the love of music is concerned, you could design a room completely for that and select the most appropriate decorations.

In both of these examples, you are making a decision about the design based on your whether or not a certain purchase will get you closer or further from what you are trying to achieve. You are also considering if a certain decision will bring joy or not. You also begin to include more dimensions into your decision-making process such as an opportunity cost and whether a purchase of something is an objective improvement.

When you think like this, then it will be much harder for you to be influenced by marketing campaigns since you clearly know what you want and you won't be satisfied until you are successful in achieving that. That is easier said than done however and there are still certain urges to resist.

How to Resist the Temptation to Buy Unnecessary Clutter

When you are considering making a purchasing decision, you should have a checklist you want to run through in order to determine if a certain purchase will improve your lifestyle. Think about the long term implications of the purchasing decision.

It is also very helpful if you are educated about all the small subtle tricks which marketers tend to use in order for people to spend their money on something for which they didn't even know they wanted. When you are about to buy something, you want to use that as a trigger to slow down and to think through your decision. Most of the purchases are made emotionally and by slowing down, you can protect yourself from being too impulsive for your own good. The solution in this situation is to think logically and rationally about what you really need for your situation and by doing this over a course of time, you will be surprised at the improved quality of your decisions.

If you are going to buy something, then have a plan for the purchase beforehand and by doing so, you will not be making purchases on the spot. Whatever you were thinking about buying will likely be there and if you determine that that same thing is actually valuable, then you can go ahead with the purchase.

Have a List

There is a way to resist the temptation of buying new shiny stuff, and that is having a list of things that you really want to do. You may think that this is redundant and that you can easily keep track of everything, but the fact is that people are forgetful and that there are a lot of things that tend to get left unattended such as books that were never read or recipes that were never tried out or various activities that never seem to get their turn to be tried out. These activities can be anything from learning a new language to catching up with an old friend.

It can be easy to forget about all these things when some free time finally becomes a reality and then it can be easy to follow the path of least resistance and to simply slump in front of the TV.

It really may not be necessary to buy a new book when there are so many other books that are waiting to be read. Instead of working away in order to save money for a new TV, it can be good to remind yourself of the joy of simply going to a park or to a newly opened museum. Having a list where your ideas for an evening are listed is a really useful strategy. You can turn to that list every time you get the urge to buy something and by doing this, you will come to the realization that there are plenty of options already in your vicinity which don't require spending money, or at least not as much. You should look at your home as an ally on your path to your goals.

Chapter 17: Declutter & Organize The Bath Areas

Declutter/Organize the Bathrooms

Keep your goal in sight. You are attempting to maximize the bathroom space and make everything accessible and easily reached by all family members. Sometimes, it is not an easy task to find a one-plan-fits-all solution. However, these are some of the tips to help you with the process:

Group the Items

If you have a stockpile of products such as extra hair care products, group them together in an organized manner. If you have three partially used bottles of the same shampoo or conditioner, mix the similar products and toss/recycle the extra container. Be sure to check under the cabinet and in the shower stall.

Drawers: Remove all of the items from the bathroom drawers and place them in containers for sorting. If an item is obviously trash, throw it away immediately. At this point, don't linger on an item. Clean the drawer, so it can thoroughly dry overnight.

Countertops & Sinks: Use the same procedures as used in the kitchen space. It will depend on the material used on the sinks and countertops.

Medicine Cabinet Purge: You already have the medicine cabinet empty from giving it a thorough cleaning; now it's time to do the tedious job of checking the dates of the medicine from the cabinet. Throw away all expired prescriptions or over-the-counter medicines. If you have any ointments, also check for spoilage of them.

As crazy as it sounds, your medicine should not be stored in the bathroom because the vitamins and medicines can become damaged from the steam and heat from showers. Place them in the kitchen instead - just for safety purposes.

Store your antiseptics, bandages, gauze, or other first aid items in the medicine cabinet. You can use it to store extra swabs, nail clippers, or any smaller items. Consider placing your toothbrushes in the cabinet to keep them more sanitary.

Place a couple of hangers on the linen closet door for hanging blow dryers, curling irons, or extra towels. It all improves the appearance of the bathroom.

Regroup The Linen Closet: Go through the cabinet/linen closet and discard any torn or dingy towels or washcloths. You can reuse the damaged ones for cleaning rags. Remember Grandma's saying, 'Waste not; want not.'

Store the extra toilet paper on the top shelf, out of the way of the regularly used items such as towels. You can also purchase a toilet paper stacker to save space.

Prepare an All-White Linen Closet

If your decluttering plan is part of the redecorating scheme; considering using all light color sheets, towels, and pillowcases. Designers believe it is more soothing to save the splashy colors for the throw pillows, blankets, and shower curtains; just a thought!

● HINT: If you have special linens and towels for guests; consider placing them in a plastic bin. Label them for easy access.

The Shower Curtain

It is beneficial to use a shower curtain liner made from cotton, hemp, synthetic, or vinyl. While you are deep cleaning, either replace the liner or machine wash it in hot water using a mild laundry detergent. Washing the liner weekly will help prevent the buildup of mold or mildew. If you prefer to hand-wash the liner, use ten parts of water to 1-part bleach.

Clean the outer shower curtain by following the manufacturer's instructions or in warm/hot water with a mild detergent.

Note: Leave the shower curtain closed when it is not being used so water cannot sit in the folds.

Limited Bathroom Space Solutions

If you are limited in space as many people are living in smaller homes, use an over the door shoe organizer. Purchase one that is clear, so you can place many items in the unit and know exactly where it is when it is needed.

Use a rule of thumb and corral any of the items that won't stack easily. Consider using small bins that can be stacked under the sink or in the drawers for makeup, and other small items that you can never find.

Place cotton swabs (Q-tips), cotton balls, and similar items in closed containers to keep them clean, organized, and out of the way.

Label the Shelves

If you have several shelves containing miscellaneous items, you can avoid a lot of digging/searching later. You can use masking tape or a label maker, to keep the children involved. Not only is it neater, but also a lot less time is spent with wondering where a certain item is when it is needed.

Refresh the Space

To finish off the bathroom space, add a box of baking soda in the corner of the closet to absorb any of the musty odors which can collect.

Corral the Children's Bath Toys

You can use several containers for the children's playtime adventures. You can use a milk crate or plastic laundry basket for the items. It will keep they neatly stored behind the shower curtain. If you want them hidden away in a closet, be sure they are completely dry to prevent mildew.

Under-the-Sink Storage

If you have limited space under the sink, it is probably best to remove everything first. Go through each article to decide if it's still needed; if not, toss it. Use a metal rack and store smaller things you may need in the lower section of the cabinet space. After you declutter, you can reorganize all the stuff. Put away the items that do not belong there. Just remember, you will need to quickly remove the items if you have a plumbing emergency. That's why it's important not to have it packed to the max.

Chapter 18: Minimalist Eating/Dieting

Can you take your minimalism to the next step? The things you eat can also adapt to fit a more minimalistic approach. Before you start any dieting or change to your eating habits—visit a physician and discuss your options and what you hope to attain from your lifestyle changes.

There is one important rule to food and water intake per day—you should never eat less than 1,000 calories and you always need to drink at least six 8-ounce glasses of water per day. This rule is for your health. People often think that eating less than 1,000 calories per day in healthy or even minimalistic eating, but it is not.

Eating less than 1,000 calories a day, according to several nutritional experts, is akin to starving your body. Your mind will realize you are not getting enough food to use for energy. It will start to hoard food, which is why you can gain weight when you are eating less than 1,000 calories per day. Whatever you eat is used for energy and whatever is left is stored as fat to be used slowly for energy.

The answer is not to starve yourself with "minimalist" eating techniques, but to truly understand what healthy eating means. Should you sit down and eat 2,000 calories in one sitting? No, but you should eat a healthy amount of food based on your current height and weight. Your doctor can explain what a healthy intake of food is per day for your height, weight, and any health conditions you may have.

Your weight and whether you need to lose or gain weight is always based on the body mass index for your age and height. A person who is five feet two inches should be around 105 to 136 pounds to be at a healthy weight and BMI. Someone who is taller, say five feet eight inches can weigh over 140 pounds and up to 160 as long as the BMI is not showing overweight or obese.

Another factor about weight is the difference between fat and muscle. Muscle weighs more than fat. It is possible someone with a very low BMI could weigh more than the standard pounds set by health organizations because of their muscle mass.

Now that you understand your health a little bit more, what exactly is minimalist eating or dieting?

Dieting is such an ugly term because we often take it to mean that we are on a perpetual diet versus establishing healthy eating habits that adapt our lifestyle. Think of minimalist eating as a way to change your lifestyle, so that still enjoy what you eat, without leading to health complications.

You have a few choices in how you approach healthy eating as a minimalist. You can make it more like a diet, where you count your calories and weigh yourself religiously. An alternative is to watch the portions you eat while ensuring you always have a well-balanced meal.

A well-balanced meal is one where you have something from every food group— yes—despite what many people it is about making sure you have a food from each of the food groups. You need protein, vegetables, fruits, grains, and dairy products. These categories are where your body gets its energy. The national health organization considers the five food groups to be the following:

carbohydrate

proteins

dairy

fruit and vegetables

sugars and fats

Carbohydrates are mostly starchy fruits, vegetables, and grains. Potatoes, bread, grain cereal, oatmeal, and rice are a few of the starches. Carbohydrates have energy created from breaking down the carbohydrate and turning it into glucose. Fats and sugars are also helpful for your brain since they offer glucose; however, you want to avoid a high fat/sugar content in your diet. While you get glucose; therefore, energy, you also gain fewer nutrients that will sustain your body throughout the day.

Shopping for your Meals

Deciding to adopt a minimalist lifestyle is about saving where you can, bringing less into your home, and remaining healthy. When you decide to choose the minimalist eating habits, you are not going to starve yourself, but you are going to make more dishes with less.

You might decide to grow your own vegetables and fruits. It is a sustainable option, while also helping you save money on meals. Growing your own food ensures you have a continual supply of that food, without spending more than it takes to obtain the plants, soil, fertilizer and containers/land for the plants. Many of the plants will continue to produce without needing to be replanted. However, root vegetables do need to be replanted every few weeks. The best part is a number of seeds you get in a seed package. You get plenty of seeds to continue to replant and all it takes is 0.99 cents to $2.48 for the seeds.

If you are not a gardener, do not have a lot of room, or the urge to grow your own plants, then learning to shop with savings in mind is imperative.

Always go to the store with meal plans.

Know exactly what you need to buy.

Know the layout of the store to avoid trouble areas, such as processed foods and baked goods.

Planning your meals helps you buy the groceries you need for the week. You may need to change your eating habits, so you are not giving in to your cravings; however, you will ultimately eat better if you plan meals.

Some individuals will take the 30 minutes it takes to plan meals, and have an alternative meal. With eight meals to choose from, it allows the person to make something that sounds good that day without going back to the grocery store.

You can still keep a few things on hand. Buying bulk meat is a good idea if you have a large family in order to keep your costs down. However, if you do not have the storage for a lot of food, then choosing the meat you eat the most and having smaller portions of what you do not eat a lot of is one way to keep your kitchen in a minimalist condition.

Another way to keep from making excessive purchases when you are at the grocery store is to shop with cash. If you walk in with a certain amount of cash, then you know you cannot buy things that look good to you now, without compromising on something later.

The takeaway from this information is to ensure that you are using a few ingredients, spending less time on cooking, and yet eating a well-balanced meal. Crockpot meals are one of the best ways to lower the cooking time on meals you eat. You also have NuWave, Dutch Ovens (instant pots), and quick 10 to 30-minute meals that you can create.

Chapter 19: Maintaining A Minimalistic Lifestyle

In the previous chapter, you learned all you needed to know on how to start incorporating minimalism in your lifestyle. Next, I'd like to discuss a crucial part of minimalism that most minimalist coaches tend to overlook: maintaining that minimalistic lifestyle once you've started. Every year, thousands of seasonal minimalists begin taking baby steps toward a minimalistic lifestyle but end up sliding back into their materialistic and unproductive old habits before the month is over. Minimalism isn't a one-time process; it's a continuous one. To continue the process properly and turn it into a life-long journey, try sticking with the following practices:

Associate yourself with minimalistic people

While this advice might sound simple enough and a no brainer, I'm putting this

179

on top of the list for two simple reasons. One, it's grossly overlooked by most minimalists, and it's much, much harder than it sounds. Peer pressure has a harder grip on us than most of us imagine, so if you expect to be a minimalist among a bunch of spendthrift friends, you're mistaken.

And two, by deciding to become a minimalist, you've decided to go against the flow of social norms and standards. To ensure you don't buckle under this pressure you need to reevaluate your choice of companionship.

Making friends as children is quite easy for us unless we were particularly shy because we are aren't critical about our friends and don't have to be cautious about their intents. As adults, we know how apathetic and cruel people can be to others who don't fit their definition of normal. We must evaluate our friendships based on how useful they are to us and vice-versa. Fortunately, minimalists tend to keep their relationships genuine and simple, so you shouldn't have much trouble spotting one in a crowd. Their body language and way of conversation is open and direct; they avoid drawing attention to themselves unnecessarily unlike most sociable people around us who prefer simplicity and comfort in their attire instead of trying to be trendy and fit in. Most importantly, you won't see the tendency of pleasing people in their walk or talk; minimalists know how to hold their ground in any situation without escalating it for the worse. When you keep company with minimalistic people, incorporating the right minimalistic traits in your personality and lifestyle become much easier thanks to their living example.

Identify the reasons of clutter in your lifestyle and eliminate them

The reasons for clutter in an individual's life varies from person to person. Clutter can happen for many reasons from buying excessive gadgets, books, and hobby items that clutter up one's home. Once you're done with the decluttering process, have a seat and note down the reasons why the clutter is occurring —you might be a die-hard comic book fan who loves collecting action figures or a bookworm who impulsively keeps on buying books despite not having time to finish them. Once you have your reasons figured out, eliminate the habits that cause cluttering in your lifestyle by replacing them with a different hobby or action that will result in less clutter.

Be an avid book reader

Books may seem like an elementary form of entertainment compared to other sensory-stimulating entertainment forms like music or sports, but the true beauty of reading lies in the fact that you can process and integrate what you read at your own pace while in other entertainment forms you're entirely at the performers' mercy when it comes to pacing. If we're what we eat, then we're also what we read. Nothing molds and influences our minds and souls quite like them. To continuously sharpen and improve your minimalistic skills and mindset, keep reading useful books that contain in-depth discussions on related topics like discipline, creativity, lean processes, and more. By deep diving into these disciplines, you'll end of finding a lot of useful tips and theories that you can experiment and play around with which you won't find in most minimalism blogs, websites, and videos on Google or YouTube. Another positive side effect of becoming a bookworm is that it will allow you to cut down on unnecessary entertainment distractions which are unproductive and expensive.

Learn to use the internet properly to master DIYs

While the internet has become as vital as oxygen for most people, few know how to utilize the internet properly. If you're good with your hands if you can radically cut down on buying a lot of things as you can make them instead by watching video tutorials or on DIY sites like Pinterest. But learn to differentiate what's worth investing your time in; if you can buy a chair from a local furniture store for $40 rather than make it from Pinterest instructions costing you $70, then it's wiser to just buy it instead of trying to make it. Just because you know how to do certain things doesn't mean it's the best course of action for you.

Take cue from Eastern cultures and reorganize often

A bad tendency among many minimalists is that as soon they manage to free up some time by uncluttering and decentralizing the various elements around them, they leave it like that without planning further changes. Keep reorganizing your furniture and belongings on an occasional basis, so you don't lose touch with your ability to synergize things properly.

Reorganizing on an occasional basis also allows you to identify whether any new type of clutter is forming in your lifestyle.

Digital Minimalization

Your level of dependency on them primarily defines the difficulty of decluttering digitally. Digital minimization doesn't apply to smartphones only; PC, televisions, stereo sets, and gaming consoles are also digital devices. When I was a kid, I was addicted to watching T.V a lot which made me ignore my chores like fixing my bed and tidying up my stuff, turning my room into a messy cascade of personal stuff starting from school books to music DVDs. My mom was very adamant on raising my siblings and me into responsible and self-sufficient adults, so other than the obligatory weekly dusting and mopping she never tidied up my stuff. This forced me to adopt a minimalistic lifestyle to reduce the clutter and keep things manageable once I got into middle school.

Smartphones are replacing desktop functions with specialized apps which can perform a plethora of tasks. As smartphones tend to be a big investment for a lot of us common folk, we try to get as much utility out of them as possible, which for most people means using as many apps as possible for micromanagement, social media, reminders, scheduling, and more. I've never personally jumped into the smartphone bandwagon as I get most of my work and correspondence done on my desktop and laptop, but that doesn't mean I'm against the notion of having one as they're quite useful to people in technical and marketing professions. Most career-oriented people I know who carry smartphones tend to use six to eight apps on average regularly. At least three social media apps and about the same amount of communication and work-oriented apps along with another other entertainment apps like Spotify and Netflix. Thus, most people who use smartphones end up wasting more time on social media and entertainment apps which have the majority presence on their device. They end up leeching up our valuable time, turning us into habitual procrastinators.

One handy tip I got from a minimalist friend for digital minimization when it comes to smartphone apps is to have all your necessary apps on one page of the phone's task manager. If you need to swipe left for the next page, it's a clear indication that you're using more apps than necessary and wasting time unnecessarily.

To be honest, most people can go without smartphones. If you can get the essential functions of making and receiving calls and texts out of the cellphone, the additional features of smartphones are unnecessary and just feeds the vicious consumerist cycle we find ourselves in constantly. Have you ever wondered how companies keep on making all these apps for free without any making any revenue? The user agreement states that downloading and using those apps gives the owners the legal loophole they need to sell your personal data commercially with impunity to companies who use that data to tailor targeted advertisements for you through various social media and user-interaction based websites. Facebook alone has faced more than two major data leak scandals in the last one year that released personal data and photos of millions of users on the internet which affected smartphone users the most.

After smartphones, the next two biggest digital time killers are televisions and gaming consoles. If possible, you should throw out your T.V! With today's internet, this is no longer a problem anymore as the same shows, cartoons, and movies that can be seen on T.V can be seen through desktops and smartphone devices as well. The standard screen size of monitors and smartphone screens are now large enough that you don't have to squint. Advertisements are why I dislike T.Vs so much; when watching something on the internet on my PC or console, I at least have the option to skip ads which aren't even an issue if you have a premium subscription to channels like Netflix. T.Vs also take up a lot of space depending on its mounting options. Did I also forget to mention that the price difference between a monitor and a T.V of the same size can be almost half? This means a quality smart-monitor can easily replace your television in the living room. Considering these points, I'm sure most of my readers will agree that other than a materialistic urge to keep a big box around, there isn't any sensible reason why you should be using a T.V anymore even if having state-of-the-art gadgets and devices are a priority to you.

This brings us to the third time-killer which is gaming consoles. Though the word 'gaming' is added to the prefix, modern day consoles have evolved into the ultimate home entertainment solutions over the past decade. Consoles are so widespread these days; one out of every ten people own a console in developed and developing countries around the world, and why wouldn't they? You can play video games, use the internet, watch movies, and listen to music all with the same device which provides a better experience than the best smartphones (media and fun applications), DVD players and stereo sets put together. However, just like smartphones, console owners often also tend to over-indulge themselves with their devices. Luckily, consoles aren't as integral to our lives as smartphones, so cutting down the time spent on it is comparatively easier as you can restrict yourself from using it. Basically, it doesn't perform any vital communication or professional functions like cellphones and desktops.

Once you start digital minimization, you'll notice you're no longer using a lot of small items that used to clutter your bags such as earphones, mini speakers, camera lenses, keypads and more which will significantly reduce the small everyday clutters you have to face. The digital devices in our lives have a lot of hidden costs in terms of peripheral accessory devices which we don't even realize until the cash memos start piling up.

Chapter 20: How To Get Rid Of Paper Clutter

Do you remember the fresh, light feeling when you first moved into your home? There were so many options. And there were no papers anywhere. But six months is enough for piles of paper to build up.

Maybe you moved in only six months ago and you have a small pile of paper clutter on your counter, or perhaps you have a monumental collection of paper gained from over ten years. The process is the same, just its length will be different. Although it might feel daunting to even look at all those piles, don't let that discourage you and make you give up before you start. Here's a guide on how to declutter paper once and for all. No minimalist hoards paper clutter.

For this purpose, you will need three empty containers or boxes.

Most of the papers you have been keeping for years will be discarded in the end—you will never file or organize them. So you'll dispose of a lot of stuff and the first box, the recycle bin, should be the biggest one.

The second box is for the papers you should keep and that will be the smallest amount.

The third one is meant for all of those "I'm not sure about this" papers. Put as few papers as you can here, then label it with the date when the box should be discarded without opening, and place it somewhere out of sight. Set the re-examination date for three or six months. If it happens that you need something from it during that time, you know it's still there and can simply take it out. If you don't take back anything, just toss the whole box.

Sort all of the papers into one of those categories by deciding for each item if it is easy, medium, or hard to replace. If it's super-easy to replace, you can get a new one or you can find information online or with a phone call and you don't need to keep it.

If a paper can be replaced, but you need to take some action that could take a while, about 15 minutes or so, it's medium replaceable.

And if it's something unique, like tax papers or a marriage or birth certificate, or guarantees, definitely keep it. File it all in one place.

Let's get to some realistic examples:

Birthday cards: It's really kind of your loved ones to show you attention this way. Appreciate them, be thankful, but this doesn't mean you are supposed to keep all of the cards. You will get new ones next year. The exceptions are cards from dear people who are not here anymore. In that case, display the item.

Owner's manuals: Today, you can find all the information you could need online. It's more likely you will search for a certain piece of information on the internet than that you will ever read the manual. Not to mention the owner manuals in many different languages you get when you buy something big.

Insurance: Life insurance, health insurance, car insurance—whatever you need about insurance, you can make a phone call. It's more efficient than trying to find information in those papers. Toss them.

Magazines: If you are one of those people who actually reads magazines, enjoy them. But if that unopened magazine on your coffee table makes you feel guilty, get rid of it. If you ever have so much free time to wish you had magazines, you can always buy them or borrow from a friend or the local library.

Notes from conferences and seminars: These might be particularly useful and full of quality information. However, if haven't read these notes and they're over a year old, you don't need to keep them. They might be outdated or you can find them online.

Bills and receipts: If it's out of date, throw it away. There's no point in keeping a bill in case of returning an item that's already used.

Coupons: If you collect coupons, don't let them fly all around the house. Decide on a special place for them. It's best to keep them in your car so you can use them when you go shopping. From time to time, toss the expired ones.

And that's it. You have probably emptied the trash can a few times up to this point. File those important papers you need to keep, put the "maybe" box out of sight, and be merciless about new papers coming into your house.

How Minimalism Can Impact Your Workout Routine

Principles of minimalism can be applied to all aspects of life and can affect all the areas of your life. Exercising is not an exception. I've noticed that since I became a minimalist, my workout routine changed in terms of being more focused, more intentional, and consistent.

Here we'll talk about how to apply main minimalism concepts to exercise.

Be intentional.

First, decide on your goals, what you want to achieve by exercising. Then decide on the right approach and make a proper workout plan with help from the internet or a personal trainer. Your workout routine will be different if you want to build muscle mass, strengthen your body, prepare for a marathon, or lose weight.

Be laser-focused for the best results with the least effort.

I used to do all the muscle groups in each session. Needless to say, my training was too long and hard and I would give up my routine after some time. Now, I work out only for 30 minutes a day and I do only one muscle group a day. For instance:

Day 1 - biceps

Day 2 - triceps

Day 3 - back

Day 4 - chest

Day 5 - legs

Day 6 - glutes

Day 7 - rest

This works great for me. Try out different options and find your perfect routine that requires less effort and time in a gym, yet gives you the desired results.

Take it slowly.

Don't speed things up and don't try to impress anyone by lifting more than you can. Not only will you look like a dummy, but you can hurt yourself too. Begin with easy exercises and small weights, then progress gradually. That's the only healthy way. Otherwise, you'll burn out at the beginning and then spend weeks recovering. That's not the way to build a healthy habit.

Be consistent.

It's better to exercise for 20 minutes every day than to train for two hours on a weekend.

You don't need fancy equipment.

Working out is not a reason to create fake needs. Your own weight is usually enough. You can even do most of the exercises using a block of wood in a forest. If you go to a gym, great for you. That's enough.

Choose the activity you enjoy.

Don't force yourself to run or to go to the gym just because it's mainstream and you think you are supposed to that. Try out different things, go swimming, biking, hiking, group sports, until you find out what you enjoy the most.

A Minimalistic Diet

This might sound weird, as if you should be hungry all the time. But actually, the minimalistic approach can help you with a healthy diet too. If you apply these principles to your diet, you'll never be obese, and you'll feel healthy and energized. At least, this was true in my case. I hadn't been overweight, but my body wasn't in perfect shape and I had a few pounds more than I needed. That completely changed when I adopted my new lifestyle. Not only did I begin a new habit of working out, but I also changed my diet a lot.

Applying the main principles of minimalism to food means that you keep in your diet only real food that nourishes your body and spirit. You don't need processed sugar, soda, or junk food of any kind. Today, my diet is simple and clean: I eat a lot of fresh fruit and vegetables, poultry, fish, nuts, and seeds. And I find it's completely enough. I don't need sweets (except fruit and moderate amounts of honey), dairy, food in plastic packaging, or anything my grandpa wouldn't recognize. If it grows, have at it. If your great-grandparents would know its name, eat it. If not—you don't need it.

I've noticed that we as a society eat a lot for all kinds of reasons: when we're hungry, thirsty, upset, nervous, bored, emotionally hungry, or even if there's just a piece of something delicious available. I decided to keep only one good reason to eat: hunger. So I only eat when I feel hungry. All my other needs have to be met some other way. It required some practice and introspection, but after some time I learned to recognize my needs and fulfill them.

Your diet should be simple and your meals should not require a lot of time to prepare. Eating is not the main activity in life, but the fuel for other, more interesting things. So you need quality fuel to run your vehicle, not another complicated activity that absorbs crazy amounts of your time. Your food should serve you, not the other way round. Also, it's not wise to put vast amounts of food into your body, making it overweight, and then putting extra time and effort into making it looks better. You have to spend a lot of time and energy in the slimming process. And that's not the worst part. If you practice an unhealthy lifestyle, what awaits you sooner or later are health issued and medical help. Do you know how much energy, stress, and money that requires? It's not pleasant at all. Think about your health while you still have it. It should be one of your priorities, and what you do every day towards that goal counts.

Of course, every now and then you can eat some "junk food." You don't want to entirely have to give up small treats, dinner with friends, french fries with kids after a movie. But now those are exceptions, and I focus on the taste and enjoyment rather than just gulping down the meal. In the end, taste and pleasure are the only reasons why I eat some unhealthy but delicious bites from time to time.

Conclusion

I really hope that the information you read in this book helped you. And you could tame the most terrible monster – the Internet, and now it doesn't rule you, but you rule them.

The Internet is one wonderful, but dirty place. If you do not use it wisely, you will find yourself trapped.

And, ultimately, in this life, we have all the tools we need for convenience: alarm clocks for every taste and color, excellent modern voice recorders, lightweight and powerful cameras, compact notebooks for recordings, paperback books and electronic books with a screen that looks like a paper page, and so on and so forth. Looking at the assortment, we must admit that we love our smartphones so much not only because they replace an alarm clock or a voice recorder, but also because they tie us to themselves due to less obvious mechanisms. They are pleasant to the touch, beautiful, fragile, they easily adapt to our habits, and they are always new, and "very much ours" - filled with personal photos, records, dialogues, and addresses.

They are such because "supply creates the demand", and "demand creates supply". This is not entirely about the development of technology, and not quite about the development of society. A lot of very attentive people listen to everything we say about ourselves and about communication. After all, they need us to make a purchase, we need to provide data. They will do everything to maintain our interest since interest is profit. Are we ready to change our lifestyle so much for someone else's profit?

CPSIA information can be obtained
at www.ICGtesting.com
Printed in the USA
BVHW071532070221
599576BV00004B/225